P9-BJL-624

"WANT TO KEEP YOUR JOB, your significant other, your friends, your family? Want to keep yourself out of jail? As a former police officer and Vietnam veteran, I highly recommend *Angry Men* to every modern-day warrior, husband, father, son, boyfriend, and friend. From the first page, the book is crammed with information you can use immediately. This book will make your life easier—and better. Every man needs to read it."

—**Loren Christensen**, author of *Crouching Tiger: Taming the Warrior Within, Deadly Force Encounters, On Combat* (with Dave Grossman), and numerous other books; www.lwcbooks.com

"EVERY MAN SHOULD READ THIS BOOK. Whether the problem is your own anger, or someone else's, McClure will give you specific, easy-to-use techniques to take control. Bypass 'Don't get mad, get even'—and, instead, listen to McClure: 'Go ahead and get mad, but take control and come out ahead'."

—**Dr. Alexis Artwohl**, Survival Triangle Training, psychologist and law enforcement trainer; www.alexisartwohl.com

"I REALLY LIKE DR. MCCLURE'S format of presenting circumstances that men, all too often, find themselves in. Dr. McClure offers skills, and then applies the skills to these circumstances. I was especially impressed with the section on depersonalizing."

—**Dr. John D. Byrnes**, author of *Before Conflict: Preventing Aggressive Behavior* and President of the Center for Aggression Management; www.aggressionmanagement.com

Dedication

To all peace officers and all peace warriors,
With respect and gratitude for everything you do

* * *

To
Kevin Manvel Lewis,
at Arizona State Prison—Complex Lewis,
with love and hope:
May this book help you take *real* control of your life.

* * *

And to all men who wrestle with anger

ANGRY MEN

Managing Anger in an Unforgiving World

Second Edition

Lynne McClure, Ph. D.

IMPACT PUBLICATIONS
Manassas, VA

Copyright © 2018, 2004 by Lynne McClure. All rights reserved. Printed in the United States of America. No part of this book may be used or reproduced in any manner whatsoever without written permission of the publisher: IMPACT PUB-LICATIONS, 7820 Sudley Road, Suite 100, Manassas, VA 20109, Tel. 703-361-7300 or Fax 703-335-9486.

Warning/Liability/Warranty: The author and publisher have made every attempt to provide the reader with accurate, timely, and useful information. The information presented here is for reference purposes only. The author and publisher make no claims that using this information will guarantee the reader an anger-free life. The author and publisher shall not be liable for any losses or damages incurred in the process of following the advice in this book.

ISBNs: 978-1-57023-397-5 (paperback); 978-1-57023-398-2 (eBook)

Library of Congress: 2003103441

Publisher: For information on Impact Publications, including current and forthcoming publications, authors, press kits, online bookstore, newsletters, downloadable catalogs, and submission requirements, visit our company website: www. impactpublications.com.

Publicity/Rights: For information on publicity, author interviews, and subsidiary rights, contact the Media Relations Department: Tel. 703-361-7300, Fax 703-335-9486, or email: query@impactpublications.com.

Sales/Distribution: All distribution and special sales inquiries should be directed to the publisher: Sales Department, IMPACT PUBLICATIONS, 7820 Sudley Road, Suite 100, Manassas, VA 20109, Tel. 703-361-7300, Fax 703-335-9486, or email: query@impactpublications.com. All bookstore and eBook sales are handled through Impact's trade distributor: National Book Network, 15200 NBN Way, Blue Ridge Summit, PA 17214, Tel. 1-800-462-6420.

Quantity Discounts: We offer quantity discounts on bulk purchases. Please review our discount schedule for this book at www.impactpublications.com or contact the Special Sales Department, Tel. 703-361-7300.

The Author: Lynne McClure, Ph.D., is a nationally recognized expert in managing high-risk behaviors. President of McClure Associates, Inc., in the Phoenix area, Dr. McClure is also the author of *Angry Women, Anger & Conflict in the Workplace, Risky Business,* and *Managing High-Risk Behaviors* (video). Dr. McClure has been featured by *CNN News Stand, CBS This Morning, The O'Reilly Factor*, and other prominent media. Her clients include Fortune 500 companies and government agencies.

The line drawings on pages 124-126 are by Johnny Lewis, an artist with a keen eye for people's moods, facial expressions, and body language. He has a creative way of portraying these moods with only a few lines. Mr. Lewis lives in Phoenix with his wife, Sondra, and their children, Phillip, Jarek, and Kaleb.

Contents

What Angry Men Need to Know and Do

Seven Life-Changing Skills for Angry Men`

Make a Difference

Acknowledgments

Many people took part in making this book. I want to thank each one.

First is Lt. Col. Dave Grossman, my friend and brother warrior, whose support included godfathering the book, introducing me to the men who told their stories, and even editing some of the finer points.

To each of the men with military, law enforcement, prison, and other backgrounds, who generously donated the stories of their own "wrestling matches" with anger. The need for privacy prevents me from listing your names, but you each know who you are.

To Ron Krannich, my publisher, a man of vision who saw the need, believed in my work, and suggested the book. To Mardie Younglof, my editor, whose flexibility made everything possible. To Barry Littmann, whose artwork shines on the cover. And to Johnny Lewis, whose sketches capture the feelings.

To all my family and friends, who are more patient than one should reasonably expect.

To my parents, who taught me to love books and believe in people.

To my clients, students, and workshop participants, who truly are my teachers.

And to everyone else who tries to make things a little better – my heartfelt thanks.

– Lynne McClure, Ph.D

Foreword

SINCE THIS BOOK WAS FIRST published in 2004, anger, rage, and violence have continued to affect millions of lives each day. Some people engage in random acts of anger, such as verbal abuse and road rage, while others negatively affect close and intimate relationships through bullying and domestic violence. These toxic acts have both psychological and physical dimensions that can result in illness and death.

Whatever the origins, causes, or consequences, anger is more often than not expressed by **men** who have difficulty controlling their emotions and developing close, intimate relationships. Their dance with anger is particularly a male phenomenon that should not be confused with less expressive female anger.

As the subtitle of this book suggests, angry men increasingly face an **unforgiving world**, one that is less and less tolerant of bad behaviors in all their ugly and abusive forms, from sexual harassment to bullying to discrimination. If you have an anger issue, it's your responsible to fix it and fix it quickly or disassociate yourself from people you abuse. If you don't, they probably will. More and more people are increasingly drawing a line – cross that abusive anger line and you're headed for trouble. Indeed, as I note in *The Anger Management Pocket Guide,*

> Everyone gets angry, but some manage anger better than others. Anger, when **under control**, should be viewed as a positive and healthy emotion that helps relieve tension and stress. But it also can be an **indicator** of other **unaddressed issues** in your life, such as marital strife, financial stress, anxiety, and constant physical pain. But when anger gets out of control, it can destroy the three things you probably value the most – personal relationships, your job, and your health. Indeed, your anger may get you into **legal trouble**, from weeks of court-mandated anger management classes to a loss of property, a divorce, an arrest, a conviction, and time served in jail. In addition to creating serious physical and mental health problems (heart disease, high blood pressure, diabetes, sleep disorders, stress, depression), anger often **takes control of you**, sending you down a spiraling and self-destructive path to nowhere – a path that can have major consequences for you, loved ones, friends, and colleagues.

Angry Men goes a long way in understanding the nature of anger in men, who often engage in self-destructive behaviors and who become serial abusers of relationships. The book begins by examining what **triggers** anger in men and then extends the discussion into **seven situations** in which others manage to push your buttons. Dr. McClure quickly **moves from analysis to prescription** by outlining **seven key skills** men need to develop and practice in order to better control their anger.

I'm once again pleased to publish Dr. McClure's book on an important subject that requires increased self-knowledge, understanding, and action. I'm also pleased to have been a part of publishing her sequel for women, *Angry Women* (see pages 131 and 134). As she rightly points out, anger issues are not the same for men and women. They affect them differently and they deal with them differently. With the publication of both books, we have a much better understanding of what both men and women need to do in order to develop more positive and supportive relationships.

I also want to direct users to the extensive resource section outlined on pages 131-134. Impact Publications (www.impactpublications.com) has assembled a large collection of anger-related resources – books, pocket guides, kits, DVDs, curriculum programs – that focuses on this important subject. If you work with correctional institutions, which face many unique anger and rage issues, you'll find several resources designed specifically for these institutions and their populations.

Ronald L. Krannich, Ph.D.
Publisher and Author of
The Anger Management Pocket Guide
and 100+ other titles

Foreword

Nothing is so strong as gentleness; nothing so gentle

as real strength.

—Francis DeSales

My father once told me that a true "gentleman" was a *man* who was capable of being *gentle*. As far as he was concerned, a male who could not control his anger was not gentle, and he was not a man. My dad was a military veteran, had served a tour with the CIA, and spent most of his life as a cop, starting on the beat and retiring as a chief. He knew what it meant to be a man.

Over the years, I have been a paratrooper, a sergeant, a U.S. Army Ranger, an infantry company commander, and a West Point psychology professor. For almost a quarter of a century, I led U.S. soldiers on operations around the world. Today, I am the author of the books *On Killing* and *On Combat*, which are used by warrior organizations worldwide. I travel almost 300 days a year, training military and law enforcement organizations. I have trained elite warriors from the FBI, the Green Berets, the U.S. Navy SEALS, the LAPD, SWAT, and many, many others.

In working with all these elite organizations, I have come to learn that my dad was right. The real mark of a man is his ability to control his temper. If you cannot control your temper, then you are not a man. But "if you can keep your head when all around you are losing theirs and blaming it on you, then you, my son, are a man."

I sincerely believe that the world today is more demanding, more stressful, and more unforgiving than it has ever been in history. Managing anger in this unforgiving world is a key survival skill, and that is what this book is all about.

We have cause to be angry.

We face lies, hypocrisy, cheating, injustice, grudges, unfairness, wrong-doings, betrayals, deceit, defiance, rejection, revenge, misunderstandings, threats and other challenges every day.

Anger in response to these challenges is perfectly natural. But *uncontrolled* anger is absolutely counterproductive and self-destructive.

Anger can destroy your life. Even righteous anger. Not because of the anger itself, but because of how you deal with it. The more difficulty you have managing anger, the more you risk letting anger take away your money, your job, your wife, your friends—and your self-respect. In this book, you will see how easily that happens.

The greater the stress and pressure you live with, the more you need to read this book. Men with the toughest jobs—soldiers, firefighters, marines, police, state patrol, prison guards, construction workers, security guards, EMTs, emergency doctors, pilots, detectives, reporters, airport security, bosses, athletes, counselors, teachers, bouncers, and many others—need it.

Men with the toughest roles—warriors, protectors, defenders, breadwinners, ministers, fathers, even heroes—need it. Men who have gone astray—prisoners, addicts, abusers, gangbangers, drug dealers, gamblers—need it. All men—real men—must manage their anger, and they need this book.

One great thing about this book is that it teaches you how to manage *other people's* anger! Once you can manage you own anger, handling someone else's anger becomes easy. If you keep your cool, you can truly be the master of any person who loses their temper, and this book teaches you how to do that.

My book *On Killing* has many case studies of those who had to kill in combat. These case studies have been very helpful to others. *Angry Men: Managing Anger in an Unforgiving World* could easily have been called "On Anger," and it has many valuable, true stories from real men who have lost their tempers. The names and details have been changed, to protect their privacy, but the examples are real. You are going to see the characteristics that lead to losing control of your anger. And of your life. How manly is that?

This book will show you how to get on top of your anger, give it its rightful place and attention, and take control of your life. I commend it to your attention.

—*Dave Grossman,* Lt. Col., U.S. Army (retired).
Director, Killology Research
Group, www.killology.com
Author of On Killing, On Combat,
and *Stop Teaching Our Kids to Kill*

1

What Triggers Men's Anger?

Before you begin, ask yourself these questions:

- Do *small* things set you off real easily?

- Do you get angry real *fast*?

- When you're angry, do you *hit* the person (or an object)?

- Do you get *real* angry if someone blames you for something you didn't do?

- Do you get *real* angry if someone doesn't see your point of view?

- When you get angry, do you get even with the person in ways they won't find out about until *later*?

- When you're angry, do you feel *out of control*?

- Do you like to *get high or drink* to control your temper and ease your stress?

- Have people close to you said that you say *weird things* when you're mad?

- Do you keep your anger *inside?*

- Do other people get angry at *you* in any of these ways?

You're angry for many reasons. All of them are good reasons. And men often take out their anger physically—right then, or later.

Anger can come from a lot of sources. Read these examples. Study them. Think about what these men could have done. Later in the book, we'll look at each example again and find solutions that will work.

Jealousy can lead to anger—and so can a sense of injustice

When I was in Korea, an Army Captain was in love with a Korean girl who was a whore. She worked at a place the soldiers called Hooker Hill. Apparently he had told himself, "She's not that kind of hooker."

One night, after getting drunk, he went to visit her at work.

He walked in and saw her sitting on another guy's lap. The guy's hand was up the skirt of his "girlfriend." The Captain grabbed her by the arm and dragged her outside and down the street. He was dragging her violently, and at one point had her in a headlock.

This was all in plain view of both Korean and U.S. Army police. (Yes, the MPs watched soldiers enter and leave known brothels on a daily basis—the restrictions were never enforced.)

The MPs approached the officer and told him he had to stop what he was doing or he'd be arrested.

"You can't talk to me like that!" he shouted. "I'm a Captain in the ___ MP Brigade. I work for Colonel___. You can't touch me!"

The Captain, off-duty and drunk, was over six feet tall and more than 200 pounds. He was yelling in the face of the MP and poking him in the chest. The MPs wound up beating him down on a public street with their police batons.

But you know what? He got away with it. The Colonel "tossed him around" a little, but the Captain got off without any formal punishment. He'd assaulted a Korean girl in front of the police. He'd assaulted an MP from his own unit. But in the end, the Colonel protected him.

Sometimes you understand, but still can't stop yourself from taking out the anger anyway

It was one of those road rage things. A guy in a black Camaro cut me off and damn near ran into me. He was driving so fast I couldn't keep up with him, even though I tried. And he was doing it on purpose, I could tell. As fast as he was going, I felt like he had singled me out to pass. He pulled up and slid in front of me. I probably wouldn't have tried to catch him if I didn't know he had picked me out of all the cars on the road.

But here's the best part. A few days later, there he was again on the same freeway. I recognized him right away. This was my big chance. How often do you get a chance like that? I gunned the car as fast as it would go, got right up there next to him just like he'd done to me, and pulled right in front of him.

He tailgated me at 95 miles an hour. I had a hard time getting away from him.

Sometimes anger is easy to come by in your job

A radio call went out early in the morning: "Officer needs backup at _____." Everyone responds, and when I arrive there are already 3 or 4 units there. Officer X has a belligerent drunk handcuffed and the other units are dealing with the drunken passengers.

Officer X's drunk is seated on the edge of the rear seat, his legs and feet outside the car. He's refusing to put them inside. He just doesn't want to go to jail. He's not kicking, thrashing, or being aggressive. He's just refusing to put his legs in the car and go to jail.

Suddenly, Officer X pulls out his baton and starts beating on the man's legs and knees. The officer's face was bright red, and he was screaming and swearing as he swung his stick, THWACK, THWACK.

The drunk isn't doing anything but screaming in pain as the blows keep coming.

Officer X has totally lost it. I'm thinking he's going for the man's head next. I grab Officer X and pull him away. He loses his balance and tumbles backwards. Suddenly, he's coming after ME!

He's screaming and yelling, "Don't EVER touch me, you son-of-a-bitch! Don't EVER touch me!"

I try to explain why I pulled him off, but he's still pumped.

I retreat back to my car. Officer X eventually turned away and calmed down. Other officers got the drunk inside the car during this drama.

Nothing ever came of the incident. Officer X went up the promotional ladder. He eventually became a high-ranking officer in the department. On those few occasions when we've met, neither he nor I ever discussed the incident. I've wondered if he even remembers it—but I believe he does.

Ironically, the week before this incident, we had an officer fired and prosecuted for striking a drunk driver in the mouth with his baton. This was fresh in my mind at the time.

Sometimes, the cause of your anger can feel extremely personal, even though you know better

This man in the bar was pissed, God knows why, and got in my face for no reason at all. I knew he was drunk, so I tried to ignore him. But then he started to say things, not about me, but about my wife! He said some pretty filthy and nasty things about her. He said how he knew where I lived and he'd been watching my wife for a while. He got into how turned on he got watching her and what he was going to do to her. The more disgusting he got, the angrier I got.

Now this man had no idea who I was or where I lived.

There was no way he could have ever seen my wife. I knew this as he mouthed off. Yet I started shaking, that's how angry I got. I could feel the muscles in my face twitching and my body tensing. My heart was beginning to beat harder and I had trouble talking.

I should have just walked away. This wasn't even really about me or my wife. And I knew it. But instead I hit him. And you know what's worse? I even started getting suspicious about my wife going out on me.

When you're under personal stress, challenges to your authority can bring out your anger

I had just learned of the death of a friend—a fellow officer—in a helicopter crash. He and another officer had been working an area in the mountains nearby, and as the sun was setting, my friend didn't see the power lines and flew into them.

Both men were cremated in the crash.

When I found out, I was stunned. I remember asking myself how I should respond. I remember feeling as if I couldn't breathe. But I had no desire to weep, shout, hit the wall, or anything else. I remember one officer asking me what was wrong, because he must have seen something in my face.

In any case, I didn't have time to dwell on it, because the Sheriff's Department was requesting backup and traffic-control in a remote area where they were in the process of closing down a huge "party." More than 1,500 kids were drunk.

I responded to the area call and was amazed at the number of cars trying to get to this party—there were hundreds of them. My task was to take up a position at an intersection and route the cars LEFT, away from the party on the RIGHT.

The Sheriff's Department was sweeping them out of the area and obviously didn't want more cars coming in.

To say the least, it was—in police jargon—a "cluster-fuck."

I had been in position for about five minutes. Drivers were reluctantly following my traffic-control directions and turning away from the area as directed. All had nasty comments as they passed by, but things were going as well as could be expected.

I was very tired. I was wishing all this would end. I just wanted to go home.

And then, one car stopped and nudged towards the right. I stopped it and saw that it was two young kids, female.

I approached the right side and told them, "The party's over. Turn left and leave the area."

One girl looked at the other, said something, and began to slowly continue turning to the right. I repeated my directions and again they said something to each other, but didn't move.

Then I saw that all the other cars were watching. I knew full well that if I let one car through, it would be an unstoppable torrent of teenagers. I turned up the volume and told the girls, "If you don't turn left and leave, this [my baton] is going through your window! Now get the hell out of here, NOW!"

The next thing I knew, they had gunned the engine, were turning right—and I did what I said I'd do. I slammed my baton through their rear window as they passed (nearly running over my foot). Well, glass flew all over the place. They stopped and began screaming hysterically.

About that time, another car slid into where we were, and out jumps the boyfriend. He was the last thing I needed at the scene. I yelled something to him about having one second to leave or he was going to jail for interfering. He made some verbal threats, but did in fact get back in his car and leave.

I called for a supervisor. I managed to get the now-crying and sobbing girls calmed down. I took their identification as I knew there would be lots of paperwork. Fortunately, the Sheriff's deputies had cleared out the area and the scene was stable. I returned to the office, wrote up a memo on the incident, and went home.

I don't know if you've ever tried to break a car window with a straight piece of hickory. It is damned near impossible.

It usually just bounces off. I recall my baton just passing through the glass with nearly no resistance whatsoever. I was obviously pumped up and full of adrenaline.

There wasn't, and probably never will be, any specific training that would prepare an officer for dealing with this kind of overt defiance while directing traffic. But the failure was mine. I had just heard about my friend's death in the helicopter, and I "sucked it up" and went back to work.

Later, when I asked the Captain what I should have done instead about the kids, he said he didn't know either.

Small angers can build up into big angers

The boss had favored this employee for years. There were rumors that the employee "had" something on the boss, but we never knew for sure. What we did know was that the employee was a lousy worker and the boss covered up for him.

There wasn't much we could do about it, so most of us just blew it off. But another co-worker resented the whole situation and his resentment grew every time the problem employee got away with something.

One day, the resentful co-worker lost it and threatened the problem employee.

"You get paid as much as the rest of us, but we're all doing your work for you," he said. "I've had it. You're gonna find yourself dead in the parking lot one of these days."

He's the one who got fired, not the problem worker.

Cover-ups can make you angry

Some soldiers were arrested downtown by the civilian police for allegedly assaulting a Korean civilian. They were processed and turned over to us, but they were on "hold" because the Korean authorities maintained jurisdiction over the offense. We could take no formal action to punish or investigate the assault.

Two weeks later, more facts came out. One of the soldiers, the night before he was arrested, was approached in the same downtown area by on-duty military police. The soldier was drunk. He was assaulting a Korean civilian—an old man selling flowers. To top it off, he was belligerent to the MPs, drunk, and disorderly. No report was ever made of this.

The next night, when he was arrested for assaulting the other person, everyone kept their mouths shut. A U.S. Army staff sergeant, on-duty, in uniform, and charged with the responsibility to maintain law and order, allowed a drunk soldier to assault a Korean—the sergeant took no action other than sending the soldier on his way.

Sometimes you take out your anger on a person who has nothing to do with it

One of the men in the crew was the type that got along with everyone. You know, the kind of guy that's easygoing and doesn't let anything bother him, joking a lot and taking the pressure off everyone.

He had a favorite jacket, and we always kidded him about it because he wore it whether it was hot or cold out. One day, for no reason at all, another man on the crew—who nobody liked—took this guy's jacket and threw it into the concrete pour.

When he saw what happened to his jacket, he got real quiet and never really was the same for the rest of the time he worked with us. We missed the good times we'd had.

And for what?

You may get angry when someone gets away with things

This soldier was in the barracks getting drunk. He took a permanent marker and wrote the words "You nasty ho" on the door of a female soldier across the hall. She was in the same battalion, but in a different company.

This incident wasn't reported. Nobody said a thing. But the story came out a week later. I sat down with the battalion commander—a Lieutenant Colonel—and the Command Sergeant Major, and told them about this. I was ordered to take no action. The CSM said, "Maybe she really is a nasty ho."

On top of that, the battalion commander didn't want any heat because he already was getting negative attention from his boss because of other similar problems in the battalion. He didn't want to risk more exposure.

So an incident of sexual harassment and vandalism was allowed to go unpunished because it might make him look bad.

And here's what happened some months later. The same soldier was out drinking to celebrate his last night in the unit. He was in the club on the base and he punched a girl and knocked her unconscious.

The MPs responded and took him in. The new company commander dropped all charges.

"When he gets on that plane," he said, "he's not our problem anymore."

Being "set up" can make you angry

My boss makes himself look good by blaming everyone else for his mistakes. I was on a team in charge of setting up a new computer system. We did the technical installation, after all the decisions were made and the equipment had been picked.

When things didn't work as well or as smoothly as they were supposed to, my boss blamed my team. But the truth was that he had failed to do all the research he was supposed to do—who needed what kind of services, which types of equipment worked best together, you know, all the important stuff you have to know before you can make good decisions about computers.

If he'd gotten all the information, the decision-makers would have chosen different equipment. But the technical team got blamed for problems that really came from buying the wrong stuff.

The worst part is, you have to be pretty technical yourself before you can understand what the real problem is. To most people in the company, the team looks like we don't know how to do our jobs.

So you know what I did? I made sure my boss's computer had the worst problems. If he's going to complain about us anyway, I'll give him good reason to complain!

Your anger can affect your judgment

I was in charge of a detail to provide traffic control for an annual event. The road also led to a big park. The temperature was hot and humid.

Traffic backs up. People drink at the park and at the fair. The country roads are clogged with hot, angry drivers. At least four major accidents occurred here per day, making law enforcement nearly impossible. Most days, we ran around scraping people off the road and then writing the report.

Near sunset, at the intersection, I was directing traffic. This was a four-way stop and sorely in need of a traffic light. People do not like to wait in line—especially after a long hot day in the sun and a few beers. They do crazy stuff.

Directing traffic is a special kind of hell for a police officer. It's not real police work. You're a target—both emotionally and physically—in the middle of an intersection. You need to have lots of psychic energy and attention. It's physically draining.

All my crew had left the detail. We'd thought the bulk of the traffic was gone. But I made one last check of the intersection. It was backed up about two miles—to a notoriously dangerous area. Someone will get hurt up there, I thought.

I also thought of my wife and kids at home, my tired body, and my frayed nerves. But I stayed and finished my job anyway.

Something wasn't right. Traffic so heavy this late. I kept directing traffic and it still wouldn't go away. Then I saw three motorcycles driving on the wrong side of the road, passing all traffic. They were approaching my position.

Ah! Finally, a chance to do real police work, I thought. I'd hammer these guys, get all three. If I'm lucky, they'll run and I can go in pursuit. Wouldn't that be fun!

I directed them to the right shoulder. Next, to the police car where I felt safe, and my "pinch" book. I was charged. I remember the extreme excitement. Heart pounding, shaking at the edge of control. Of course, I didn't pay attention to what it meant. I was trained not to trust emotions. One must be in control at all times. I had been a police officer for about five years, and was confident.

I also was confident about my ability to control suspects—even three of them. They all pulled over. The leader rode up next to me and remained astride his bike. The other two held back and dismounted about 20 feet away.

Enforcement tactics now were in the shitter. With three violators who were split, I was in a bad position. They could have just robbed a store, for all I knew, and could be pulling weapons out of their leather jackets.

The leader grinned as he said, "What's the problem, Officer?"

I remember raising my voice—something I had never done with the public before. I remember his grin falling from his face.

I asked him for his license and registration. He regained his composure, smiled again, and slapped me on the stomach with the back of his hand.

"Take it easy," he said to me. "This is just a big game, you know."

Things get real fuzzy for me here. I remember impressions.

The violator said, "You wouldn't be so tough without that badge." I took my badge off and threw it into the police car.

The violator said, "You wouldn't be so tough without the gun." I took off my gun-belt, with weapons, and threw it into the police car.

The violator—not grinning anymore—said, "What are you going to do, beat me up?"

I said, "This is not a game. Get off your bike and give me your license."

The violator—with a look of shock on his face—said, "I think you would beat me up. And probably enjoy it, too."

I said, "You bet your fucking ass I would. Now give me me your license and shut the fuck up." My voice was just below rage. It felt so good to finally stand up and show someone how I really felt.

The other two quickly jumped on their bikes and left. I wrote the man a citation. I felt naked and powerful, not needing those symbols of power.

But the ticket was just another act of stupidity, because now the man had written proof of our encounter. He could easily cause the end of my promising career.

On the way home, I felt fear and guilt. Just two more emotions to stuff.

Lies and cover-ups can make you angry

There were new soldiers in the battalion who had not yet qualified on their weapons. This is a readiness problem that needs to get fixed. The company commander arranged for these soldiers to go to a marksmanship range with the brigade headquarters company. This is common practice—we often share ranges to help everyone out.

The battalion commander found out, however, and would not allow it. His justification, at a staff meeting that included his key subordinate leaders, was: "If our soldiers go to that range and do something 'wrong', the brigade commander might see them. That will make us look bad."

He was really talking about himself, of course. What is the lesson the subordinate leaders are supposed to learn from this? He would rather let the unit's wartime readiness suffer than risk "looking bad."

You may get angry when your performance reviews at work are unclear

I've had this job for five years, and every performance review is the same. I "need to be more professional" or "need improvement" in some area, but it's never clear exactly what that means I'm supposed to do.

When I ask my boss, all he says is more of the same general things. "You know, do a better job with our customers" or "Handle that problem more professionally." When I ask him what "a better job" or "more professionally" would look like, he gets angry and tells me to "stop avoiding the issues."

He's got no right to get angry. But I do! So I just stick to my job duties and don't do a single extra thing.

Sometimes anger comes from people thinking they are the "exception to the rule"

One day, after 9/11, the Colonel's wife was waiting in line at the gate. All security was tightened and the gates were under heavy guard.

The wife was displeased about the wait and the fact that she was being treated like everyone else. She gave the MP at the gate a piece of her mind. Afterwards, she called her husband.

The Colonel immediately called the MP's supervisor and relieved him of his duties—right there in front of his soldiers. There was no investigation or questioning. The only cause was the irate phone call from his wife.

Sometimes anger comes from being silenced

My company drug-tested all applicants and also current employees whose behavior was questionable. My department kept drug-test results on file.

In doing my job, I ran across a report that was inaccurate. It stated that the individual—an applicant—had tested negative for all the drugs, but I remembered that she actually had tested positive for cocaine.

When I told my boss about the error, she looked away and said, "No, that's not true. You remember it incorrectly."

I started to tell her about the original report, which I'd seen a few days after the applicant filled out the forms, but my boss looked at me and said, very firmly, "That is not correct. You must be thinking of a different report or another applicant."

I wasn't surprised to find out later that the applicant was the daughter of one of the executives. But I was angry that the executives could get away with making an exception that put everyone at risk—and that my boss was in on the cover-up.

So I told everyone who would listen, including the people who write the company newsletter. And—can you believe this?—suddenly I'm told that my job is now on third shift. They've done all the paperwork to justify the move, but you know the real reason is to shut me up.

Lack of professionalism can make you angry

During my first month of company command, the Army changed headgear from the old "patrol cap" to the new black berets as part of a symbolic transformation.

On a Friday afternoon, my operations sergeant held a class for the younger soldiers. The purpose of the class was to teach them how to wear the new hat properly—it's not as simple as just putting it on your head. I was at a staff meeting, but I trusted the staff sergeant to do a good job.

A week or two later, everyone wore the new berets for the first time at a rehearsal for our "transformation ceremony."

None of the young soldiers had prepared their berets, and none of them wore the berets properly.

I took the staff sergeant aside and asked him why the soldiers had problems with the berets, following the class.

"It's common now, Sir," the staff sergeant replied. "You know soldiers never pay attention when they're getting a class."

I absolutely lost it. I was shocked that a professional soldier could say these words out loud. I went off on him bigger than shit. It seemed hypocritical to me for a so-called leader to even think this way.

Sometimes, anger goes inward—whether or not you even know it

I'd been a surgeon for more than 30 years. I'd taught medical students how to perform surgeries. I'd written papers and spoken regularly at professional conferences. I was seen as an expert in my field.

But I started to notice some changes. They were small changes—very small. And they only happened once in a while, not all the time. But they were still important changes, and problems for me. I'd feel down, almost depressed, for no reason at all. It didn't happen very often. But it stayed with me longer than I was used to. Nothing sharp or strong. Just a generally low kind of feeling.

Then I started to feel changes in my hands. It was nothing anyone else could see, and I still did excellent work in the operating room. You couldn't tell from watching me work. But it was a new feeling inside my hands. I can only describe it as kind of a looseness, a tiny but nagging feeling of not having total control. My hands were still steady—but they didn't feel that way to me.

I felt scared. Depressed. Shocked. On the verge of being out of control.

I didn't know what was happening to me. Not knowing made everything worse. And I didn't miss the irony, either—the well-known doctor couldn't diagnose himself.

I felt caught in a whirlwind. Losing control made me more depressed. The depression made me feel more out of control. I kept going over and over it in my mind, asking myself what might it be, when did I first noticed it, what might it mean. I was afraid to tell my patients. I was afraid they'd lose faith in me. I didn't even know what to tell them. I didn't know what was happening.

When I finally saw my own doctor, it was diagnosed as early stages of Parkinson's disease. My wife, my family, felt shocked, scared, out of control. Just like I'd been feeling. But for me, the diagnosis was a relief. I finally knew what was going on.

But here was the shock for me. It wasn't until then that I realized how angry I'd been. As aware as I'd been of my fear, shock, and depression, I hadn't realized how much rage I'd also felt. About being out of control. About having symptoms I couldn't diagnose. About not knowing what was going on. I'd kept the anger inside, hidden even from myself. And the stress from all this bottled-up anger might have increased the degree, or progression, of the disease.

Defiance can cause anger

My son was 16 then. I knew damn well he was going out with his buddies to drink and do drugs. So I locked him in his room that night. I told him that if he even thought about sneaking out, I'd beat the shit out of him.

Well, next thing I know, he's gone. Went out through the bedroom window. I was pissed. SO pissed that I thought about hunting him down. But you know what? I didn't even know where to go look for him.

So I waited up all night. I got angrier by the minute. He didn't get back 'til the next night. Like he thought he could sneak back in and I wouldn't notice he'd been gone.

Well, I'm not as dumb as he thinks I am. I waited and waited, getting angrier every minute. Then that next night, I heard a car pull up across the street. His buddies must've thought they'd make me think they were someone else, stopping at the neighbor's.

I went outside, stood at the door, and just waited for him to walk up. He looked like hell. I could see him trying to make up some lies as he walked towards the door.

I didn't say a word. As soon as he got close enough, I punched him a few times. Real hard. Really walloped him—he fell back and hit his head against the tree. He broke his nose and got a brain concussion.

Now I'm being accused of child abuse. What the hell—he's the one who caused it! I told him what I'd do if he snuck out!

Even defiance from a *female* can cause anger

I think of myself as an open-minded kind of father, you know, wanting my daughter to tell me the truth about what's going on.

But I do have my limits. When I found out she was pregnant—at 15 years old, if you can believe that—I blew up.

I told her I'd rather see her dead than be the slut she is.

I slapped her too, good and hard. I asked her what the hell she thought she was doing, living in our house, letting us pay for her slutty half-undressed clothes, and acting like a whore. You'd think she was in one of my porn magazines! No wonder she's so popular with the boys!

Let me tell you, as soon as I find out who the father is, he'll get it from me too. Wait till I get my hands on him!

Sometimes fear of losing control can cause anger

My wife and I had it pretty good for a while, but then she decided to get a job. I don't know why, because we have what we need with just me working. And I think a wife and mother should stay home. But she got real moody and nagged me about it for a long time, so I went ahead and gave her permission to get a job. It had to be close by, and she had to work only with women, you know, for safety reasons.

Well, that was just the beginning. The next thing was, she decided she should save a little of her money in her own account. I thought this was kind of silly, especially because all these years, all of my money went to us, the family. But I know she never really had anything of her own, so it didn't seem like such a big deal.

Then, after a while, she got bored and got another job elsewhere. I didn't even know she'd been looking. But it was a sales job, and some of the other salespeople were men. This bothered me, and once in a while, say during lunch, I'd stop by to see her at work, just to make sure things were okay.

And they sure looked okay, until suddenly, one day, bam! Just like that, she decides she wants a divorce. What would my family think? My friends? My co-workers? Sure, I have my faults like everyone else, but a divorce? I was shocked.

And I was furious, also. I knew it was one of those salesmen, even though she denied it. I tried real hard to find out— I pinned her against the wall, I slapped her, I made her tell me who it was. She kept claiming it was no one, just her own need, whatever that means.

She even said it was my fault, because I've hit her a few times. You know what? I only hit her when she does something that deserves it. It's not my fault, it's hers. If she'd gotten that straight, there never would have been any problems.

So you see what a little independence can do to a woman. I'm not done, you know. I'll find out who it is. I have a private detective on the case right now. And when I find out who it is, they'll both wish she had never left.

Something you may not expect: anger and *shame*

It was graveyard shift. Some officers thrive on this shift. Others, like Officer X and myself, "volunteer" once every year or two.

I'm driving. It's about 3 a.m. This is drunk-watch. I hated drunks. My mother was an alcoholic, as was my grandmother. I felt a low simmer of resentment when I had to deal with these citizens. At one time, I liked throwing them in jail. By now, though, humiliating them had lost its shine. They all smell alike and they all say the same things. They were angry, manipulative, whining drunks.

Officer X observed a yellow Corvette get on the freeway ahead and alerted me. I accelerated to about 90 mph to close the distance. Traffic is extremely light. The Corvette started to pull away. I accelerate to about 120 mph and close a bit. Even with light traffic, I'm driving at the edge of my abilities. The Corvette pulls away momentarily, then slows to 110. I pull in behind at 110+ and "light" him up.

Officer X is bracing himself. It's been a short but wild ride. My adrenaline is pumping. I remember lights being brighter and colors vivid and my well-oiled hypervigilance deactivated as we pulled to the narrow right shoulder. My vision was narrow and too focused.

Ordinarily, there should be communication between the two partners on how to proceed in this dangerous situation. What level of tactics should be used, etc. This did not occur, because I was pumped.

I approached the Corvette on the left side. A tactical error and extremely dangerous. First, I had to stand in the traffic lane, due to the narrowness of the right shoulder. Second, indications were that this was not just another speeder. This situation called for a cautious approach where we might stay behind the cover of our car and use the public address system to talk to the violator, with his back to us.

We didn't do this.

The driver looked up at me and said, "What's the problem, Officer?" with a stupid grin on his face. I did not think this was a joke.

I don't remember much after this. I do remember flashing back to some locker room bravado I'd heard. One of my comrades was reporting how he'd pulled some guy out through the driver's window. I was sizing up this driver to see if I could pull him out through the window. I remember being surprised at his weight and that he wasn't fitting very well through the window. His head and shoulders outside with me and the rest somehow stuck. His screaming in fear.

I let go, opened the door, and dragged him down the traffic lane, stopping between his car and the police car.

Once he was on the ground in front of me, I had no idea what to do. As I think back now, I was shocked and sort of wondering how we got here.

At that moment, Officer X grabbed me and gently told me to stop. He turned to the violator, picked him off the ground, and dusted him off. He firmly warned the man not to speed, and apologized—not with words, but with body language and touch. He put his arm around the man and helped him back into the Corvette.

I felt enraged. I also felt shame about losing control of what I was doing.

Anger can come from cases where you just can't win

In this type of crisis, a police officer's goal is to prevent the suspect from killing the couple the suspect has at gunpoint. But the cop has other responsibilities too, so it's not as clear as it may sound.

For example, if I shoot and kill the suspect, this would remove the risk to the couple. But some people may see this as "police brutality." That makes me angry.

On the other hand, if I "just" injure the suspect, the cost of medical treatment and a trial would cost the taxpayers more money than burying him—and there still could be a risk of him killing the couple even though he's injured. That makes me angry too.

And back at headquarters—if I "only" injured the suspect instead of killing him, some of my fellow officers would see this as weakness on my part. They wouldn't praise me for saving the suspect's life. They'd avoid me and treat me as less than a man.

Not that they would come out and say I should have killed him. No, they wouldn't say the word "kill." They'd just refuse to look me in the eye. That makes me angry too.

And then, I have my own anger to deal with. Anger about the fact that anything I did in this type of situation would be wrong, from one angle or another.

Anger is natural and real. And there's a lot out there that can make you righteously angry. It's okay to *feel* angry sometimes. But ways of *dealing* with anger can take away your power—and put *anger* in charge of your life.

You're going to find out how to make sure *you* stay in charge. We will see these case studies again, later in the book, and learn how to deal with them.

ASK YOURSELF...

1. Which of these stories remind you of times you've felt angry? (The details are different, but what feelings are the same?)

2. What types of things make you angry?

3. What are some of the ways you deal with your anger?

4. Have you ever had problems because of something you did when you were angry?

2

Take Charge of Your Own Anger

You can't change the world. You can't make all the things that bother you go away. You can't stop feeling angry sometimes. But you *can* do two things to take charge of your own anger:

- You can change how you *deal* with your anger.

- You can change how you *react* to other people's anger.

To do this, you have to ask yourself a serious question: Are you *man* enough to know the difference between what you *feel* and what you *do* about it?

The first place to start is to see the *difference* between:

What You *FEEL*
and
What You *DO*

Here's what this means:

- In most of the stories you just read, the person first *felt* angry and then, right away, they *did* something about it. They immediately went from their *feelings* to *doing* something. There was no pause, no S-P-A-C-E between the feeling and the doing. The process looked like this:

FEELDO

- You saw, in the stories, that what they *did* was pretty stupid. What they did *felt good at the time,* but hurt them later. For example, the 16-year old son will have trouble looking up to his father. The co-worker lost his job and the problem employee kept his. Even though *doing something* right away *feels* good, it ends up hurting you later.

23

- The reason they *did* stupid things is that there was *no S-P-A-C-E* between what they *felt* and what they *did.* When there's *no S-P-A-C-E* between the two, there is no time for understanding what went wrong, thinking of different ways to react, choosing the best way to react, or taking any steps that could lead to positive outcomes. *FEELDO* leaves you trapped in a corner.

- If you put some S-P-A-C-E between what you *feel* and what you *do,* it will look like this:

FEEL   DO

or

FEEL   DO

or

FEEL   DO

- You get the idea. If there's S-P-A-C-E between *feeling* and *doing,* you give yourself a chance to see how you really *feel,* think about the impact on *you,* see what choices you really have, think about where the other person is coming from, decide how much time the event "deserves" you being angry about it, think about how much anger the event is "worth" feeling, decide what kinds of outcomes would be best for *you*—and *THEN* decide what to *do.*

- You will NOT be making the S-P-A-C-E for the sake of the person you're angry at—it's for *YOU!* If the men in the stories had done this, the man in the bar would have laughed off the drunk instead of getting suspicious of his own wife. The patrol officer would have stayed in control of the bikers. The fathers would have related better to their teenagers. Things would have gone better for *all* the men in *all* the stories if they had given themselves some S-P-A-C-E between what they *felt* and what they *did.*

ASK YOURSELF...

1. Think about a time you felt angry AND did something about it that (you can see now) later turned out to be "stupid."

2. How much S-P-A-C-E was there between what you felt and what you did?

3. Looking back now, what are some other things you could have done that might have had a better outcome?

Here's the hardest part: while you feel angry, you have to catch yourself *early* enough to make the S-P-A-C-E between what you *feel* and what you *do*. This is why you have to decide whether you are *man* enough to know the difference between the two. Little kids, for example, *can't* tell the difference between feeling and doing, and as soon as they *feel* something, whatever they *do* about it seems automatic and "right" to them. That's why infants cry as soon as they feel hungry, and why they scream if they have to stay hungry for too long. They're using FEELDO, with no S-P-A-C-E between what they feel and what they do. That's okay for infants and little kids.

But *real men*—who are manly because they're *adults,* as well as being males—don't cry out or scream if they're hungry. They *feel* hungry, *then they take time to decide what to do about it,* and then they *do* something. Because they've taken time to think about it, what they *do* is usually practical and sensible.

The same is true for anger. Immature men are males who are adults in the physical sense, but are children when it comes to their feelings. They act just like little kids when they're angry. They use FEELDO, because their feelings—not their own minds, not their own judgment, not their own experience, not their own intelligence, not their own maturity, and *not their own manhood*—are in control of what they *do.* Men who are run by their feelings are just big children. A *real man* is in charge of what he does *no matter what he feels.*

Here's how to make the S-P-A-C-E between what you *feel* and what you *do.* To get good at it, *practice these steps in your mind* long before you get angry. If you practice these steps at least once a day, when you're in a good mood, they'll be easier to do when you're angry and you need them.

How to Make S-P-A-C-E Between
What You Feel and What You Do

- Pay attention to *yourself,* not the other person or situation that makes you angry.

- Pay very close attention to what you *feel—physically—*when you are angry. Anger isn't just in your mind. It's also in your body. Where do you *feel* the anger—in your face? your throat? your stomach? your forehead? Notice where, on your *body*, you feel it.

- Focus on your physical feelings. Let yourself *feel* what you feel. This will help focus on *yourself—*where your control is—instead of on the other person.

- Let your physical feelings help you accept the fact that you *are* angry, and that you have the *right* to be angry.

- Think of a question that helps you do something good for yourself. For example, you might ask yourself, "Is this action, or person, or situation *worth* getting worked up about?," or "Is it worth getting worked up *this much* about it?," or "What is it about this action, or person, or situation that *makes* me so angry?," or another question you think of. Don't *do* anything yet about your answer—just be aware of it, while you let yourself feel your anger.

- Ask yourself: "What is the most low-key, yet *powerful, manly* thing I could do that would show this person I am *not* affected by him, that he does *not* matter enough to 'fight back' with, that he does *not* have the power to make me lose control of myself?" This is how you "win"—instead of "giving in" by hitting him, or yelling, or doing whatever out-of-control thing you've done in the past, you *do* something that makes him look (and feel) less important.

For example, the road-rage driver could have ignored the other driver when he saw him again—or he could have waved hello! The "jealous" husband could have laughed (silently, to himself) about the drunk. The father could have waited until the next day to have a heart-to-heart talk with his son.

The point: After getting real in touch with the anger you *feel,* pick something low-key you can *do* that will take the power *out* of what made you angry.

By following all these steps, you make a S-P-A-C-E between the anger you *feel* and what you *do.* In this S-P-A-C-E, you find ways to *do* things that take away the other person's power—and give yourself more.

Be sure to practice these steps when you *don't* need them, so you'll be good at using them when you *do* need them.

When you can separate what you *feel* from what you *do—*and you can put a S-P-A-C-E between them—you have mastered the first part of taking charge of your own anger.

You'll already be starting to change how you *deal* with your anger, and how you *react* to others' anger. There are more steps to go, but you're well on your way.

ASK YOURSELF...

1. Think of someone you know who does things that trigger your anger.

2. Think back to what you've done in the past, when you felt angry towards this person and did not put any S-P-A-C-E between FEEL and DO.

3. What would you do now, if you were in the same situation BUT you put S-P-A-C-E between FEEL and DO?

3

Seven Ways Other People Try to Control Your Reactions

Once you can put a S-P-A-C-E between how you *feel* and what you *do*, you've done something *many men can't do*. They're too macho. Many men, when they get angry, let the other person push their buttons. And they don't even know that's what's happening. But this won't happen to you. *You're* taking charge of your *own* anger. You're deciding what to do, before you do it.

The next step is to take control of your own actions and reactions in seven angry situations you've probably seen a lot. There are seven specific ways other people can trigger your anger. Each of these ways has its own trap—its own way of getting you to *do* exactly what makes the person feel like he "won" at your expense. Men who just do FEELDO will fall right into this trap. But by putting a S-P-A-C-E between what you *feel* and what you *do*, you'll be able to plan *in advance* how to deal with each specific angry situation—and its trap.

1. Acted-Out Anger

Acted-Out Anger means the person is taking out his anger physically. He might be hitting, yelling, throwing things, stomping out of the room, or doing any number of things that are easy to see and hear. His target may be a desk, chair, wall, window, TV, computer, anything physical—including, sadly, another person or other living creature. Most of the men in the stories in Chapter 1 showed Acted-Out Anger.

Acted-Out Anger's trap is that when you see how angry this person is—especially if he is acting out his anger on *you*—you will fall right into his game and start acting out your own anger as well. If you do, he wins, because he got you all worked up. He got you to *lose control* of what you *do* and fall victim to what you *feel*. It looks like this:

28

Acted-Out Anger

You get angry too,
you lose control,
you act like him.

He "wins"
because you
lost control of
your actions.

If you follow this pattern, he wins—because you're *not* in charge of what you do. *He* is. You did what *he* wanted you to do—which means he gets his way with you. If you react the way *he* wants, he'll keep using Acted-Out Anger on you.

Instead, you can avoid the Acted-Out Anger trap by:

■ putting a S-P-A-C-E between what you *feel* and what you *do*

■ *doing* things that are *very different* from his behavior

For example, instead of yelling back, you could smile, stay low-key and calm, and say, "Looks like you're getting kind of worked up. Want to settle down and talk?" Your goal is *NOT* to change him, solve everything, or win out over him. Instead, your goal is to *keep yourself out of the trap* of his anger style, and keep him from controlling you. It looks like this:

Acted-Out Anger

You're calm, detached,
and in control of what
you do.

He feels frustrated,
looks foolish compared
to you, and has no control
over you OR of himself.

The most powerful and manly thing you can do in the face of Acted-Out Anger is stay calm and in control—of yourself. When you react *your* way—*not* his—he'll stop using Acted-Out Anger on you.

2. Irresponsible Anger

Irresponsible Anger means the person is mad when you hold him accountable for something. He usually doesn't deny that the problem happened. But he blames *you* for the part of the problem that really was *his* fault. For example, you loaned a friend some money and he didn't pay you back the day he said he would. You ask him for the money, telling him he's late paying you back—and he says it's *your* fault for not reminding him!

The trap of Irresponsible Anger is that you'll believe the person and let him blame *you* for something that was *his* fault. Even if you're to blame for *part* of the problem, you are *not* responsible for *his* part. It looks like this:

Irresponsible Anger

You agree that
you are at fault for
the whole problem—
even though he is
to blame for at least
part of it.

He gets away
with not taking
responsibility for
his actions, and
you carry more
responsibility than
is fair to you.

If you react the way *he* wants you to, he'll keep using Irresponsible Anger on you. You can avoid the trap of Irresponsible Anger by refusing to take the blame for his part of the problem. If you did something that was part of the problem, you can mention it—but stick to the fact the *he* is to blame for *his* part. It looks like this:

Irresponsible Anger

You refuse to take
any of the blame for
his part—even if you
admit that you were at
fault in another way.

He can't blame you
for what he did wrong,
and he has to accept
the fact that *he* is
responsible for his part
of the problem.

The strongest way to deal with Irresponsible Anger is to stick to the facts and refuse to be blinded by his failure to take responsibility. When you react the way *you* want to, he'll quit using Irresponsible Anger on you.

3. Self-Centered Anger

Self-Centered Anger means the person's angry that he has to follow the same rules as everyone else. He's angry because he wants to be "special," the "exception" to the rule. The Colonel's wife, who tried to avoid the security guards, is an example.

Self-Centered Anger's trap is that you may find it easier to give in to them than to make them follow the rules like everyone else. If you do this, you're letting this person decide what you will do. It looks like this:

Self-Centered Anger

| You give in and treat him as "special" or the "exception"— despite what you want to do, or your values. | He gets his way, he gets you to go against what you want to do (and maybe even against your values), and he's in charge of your actions. |

If you follow this pattern, you give up control of your own actions and let the other person decide what you'll do. You also may be going against your own value system, which will make you feel even less in control of yourself. If you react the way _he_ wants, he'll keep using Self-Centered Anger on you.

Instead, you can avoid the trap of Self-Centered Anger by

- putting a S-P-A-C-E between how you _feel_ and what you decide to _do_

- refusing to treat him any differently than you treat everyone else

- reminding him that there are no "exceptions" and that no one is more "special" than anyone else

You're not trying to put him down or make him "less" than anyone else. You're staying in charge of your own actions, and doing what _you_ choose to do. It looks like this:

Self-Centered Anger

| You refuse to make an exception for him—you make him follow the rules. | He has to accept the fact that he is just like everyone else when it come to the rules—and you are in charge of your own actions. |

The most powerful and manly thing you can do in the face of Self-Centered Anger is insist on treating him the same way everyone else is treated. By reacting *your* way instead of his, you stop him from using Self-Centered Anger on you.

4. Two-Faced Anger

Two-Faced Anger means the person is nice to someone's face, but works against them behind their back. He doesn't come out and tell the person that he has a problem with them or something they did. He tells everyone else, or does something sneaky, instead. One example is the computer worker who purposely messed up his boss's computer. Another is the worker who "got even" with his boss's vague comments by being passive on the job.

Two-Faced Anger's trap is that you listen or go along with the person's anger, may agree or disagree or agree—but, just like him, *you don't tell the person* that there's a problem. "Everyone" knows that others have a problem with this person—everyone except the person, that is. It looks like this:

Two-Faced Anger

| You listen to how angry he is at the other person, and you get angry "with" him—and you don't tell the other person either. | He gains power over you, because he got you to take on his anger towards the other other person AND you kept his secret from the other person. |

If you go along with this, you're giving up your right to have your *own* feelings, make your *own* decisions, and choose for *yourself* how to deal with the other person. You've let this person *make* you take his side. And on top of that, you're *also* helping this person keep everything secret—which you know makes things get worse—instead of bringing it out in the open, where it could get fixed. Also, because you reacted the way *he* wanted you to, he'll keep using Two-Faced Anger on you.

The way to avoid the Two-Faced Anger trap is to refuse to go along with what the angry person says or does. You can listen or watch, but you can also refuse to get involved. You also can tell him that he might be better off just bringing up the issue with the person he's angry at, instead of acting it out all over the place. What you'll be doing looks like this:

Two-Faced Anger

You listen or not, but you respond in a mild way that does *not* take sides. You stay calm and refuse to take his anger on as your own.

He sees that he is on his own, and that he might be better off trying to discuss the problem with the person he's so angry at.

The way to keep your own power in the face of a person using Two-Faced Anger is to stick to your own feelings, your own issues, and your own actions. Stay out of *his* problems and *his* feelings. If you react the way *you* want to, he'll stop using Two-Faced Anger on you.

5. Rigid Anger

Rigid Anger means the person uses his anger as a way to *control* you. This is different from a friend who wants to shoot pool when you want to go bowling. With the friend, you two would just talk it over and decide. With Rigid Anger, the person yells, withdraws, badgers you, and intimidates you to get his way. He uses *power* over you.

The trap of Rigid Anger is that it's easier to give in than to argue with him. Once you give in, he'll keep using his Rigid Anger anytime you disagree with him. It looks like this:

Rigid Anger

You do what
he wants you to do,
instead of what
you want to do.

He gets *his*
way—and you
lose control of
your choices
and actions.

If you go along with this, you feel "threatened" into doing what *he* wants. You let him *bully* you into obeying him. You give him power over your choices. And you put your choices—and yourself—into a "second-rate" place. You're letting him run your life. The more you give in to him, the more he'll use Rigid Anger on you.

You can avoid the Rigid Anger trap by sticking with what *you* want to do, instead of letting *him* make your choices for you. It looks like this:

Rigid Anger

You do what
you want to do,
no matter what
he thinks you
should do.

He learns that
he can't boss
you around.

When you make your own choices, instead of letting yourself get bullied into doing things *his* way, you stay in charge of yourself. You keep your own power. You feel better and have more self-respect. Ironically, he probably will have more respect for you also—but you're still doing this for *yourself.* When you react *your* way, he'll stop using Rigid Anger on you.

6. Drinking/Drugging Anger

Drinking/Drugging Anger means either the person is angry *because* of the alcohol or drugs he's been taking, o*r* because what he's *on* has made his anger worse. An example is the drunken soldier who vandalized the female soldier's door by scrawling harassing words.

Drinking/Drugging Anger's trap is that you try to deal with the person as if he's reasonable. Under alcohol or drugs, he *isn't* reasonable—at least, not a reasonable *man*. He's more like an *un*reasonable *kid*, having a temper tantrum along with not wanting to listen. It looks like this:

Drinking/Drugging Anger

You try to talk
sense with him.

He gets more
*un*reasonable
and his anger
increases.

If you fall into this trap, you'll waste a lot of your time trying to reason with him. You'll also risk getting him angrier. Angry people on alcohol or drugs are a waste of energy. If you keep trying to treat him the way he expects, he'll keep using Drinking/Drugging Anger on you.

The way to avoid the Drinking/Drugging Anger trap is to refuse to deal with him while he's in that state of mind. It looks like this:

Drinking/Drugging Anger

You avoid
talking to him and
get away from him.
IF you talk to him,
it's only when he's
sober/straight.

He finds
someone else
to take his
anger (and
unreasonableness)
out on.

At the very least, you'll be less bothered by him, because he won't take his anger out on you. At the very best, you'll be able to talk to him when he is sober or straight. But by avoiding his Drinking/Drugging Anger, you save your time and energy for *yourself.* When you react *your* way, he'll stop using Drinking/Drugging Anger on you.

7. Delusional Anger

Delusional Anger means that what makes the person angry is *not real.* It's a delusion, or even a hallucination, in their minds. This is very different from the man at the bar who got suspicious of his wife just because of what the drunk said. The man at the bar felt suspicious, *but he knew it wasn't true.*

With a delusion or a hallucination, the person *really believes* something that you, and everyone else, *knows* is not true. Sometimes these beliefs are not even physically possible. For example, he might believe that you are physically probing his brain with wires. To the person who sees or hears them, delusions and hallucinations are much more real than a hunch or a gut feeling. Delusions and hallucinations are *just as real to them* as the physical world you (and they) see.

Because delusions and hallucinations look and sound so real to the person, it's impossible to convince them that what they think is not true. In this way, they are very much like the person with Drinking/Drugging Anger. And you should know that alcohol and drugs *can cause* delusions and hallucinations.

But some people have delusions and hallucinations even without drugs or alcohol. In these cases, it is due to mental illness or other physical problems with their brains. These people can be even worse off if, on top of their "natural" brain problems, they also take alcohol or drugs. You also should know that delusions and hallucinations come and go. The person may be very reasonable and "with it" (meaning, in touch with reality) much of the time, and very "out of it" (meaning, *out* of touch with reality) at other times.

The trap with Delusional Anger is that you *know* what they're angry at *didn't happen.* So you try to be reasonable with them, or you laugh it off. In either case, your reaction will only make them angrier. It looks like this:

Delusional Anger

You laugh him off, or you try to explain that what he thinks happened did *not* really happen.	He is even more convinced that you're out to get him—so he gets angrier, less predictable, and more dangerous.

If you go along with this, you'll waste time *and* put yourself at risk. You're trying to get him to deny something that is as *real* to him as the things *you* see and hear are to you. If you keep trying, he'll keep using Delusional Anger on you.

Because of how *real* his delusions and hallucinations are to *him,* the way out of the Delusional Anger trap is to let him know that you respect what he believes. Then, you have to let him know you did not do what he thinks you did. It looks like this:

Delusional Anger

You tell him you understand that he is angry because he thinks you did a certain thing. Then, you explain that you didn't mean it the way he took it, or you didn't know what you were doing at that moment.	He accepts that you didn't mean it the way he thought, OR he decides that he misunderstood. You are in less danger.

With Delusional Anger, you're not trying to get to the truth as much as you're trying to lower his anger in a situation where you can't win. The reason you can't win has *nothing* to do with you. It's all about *his* delusions and hallucinations—which, sooner or later, will go away and be followed by new ones. When you react *your* way, he'll stop using Delusional Anger on you.

You've seen seven angry situations that used to *make* you angry or *make* you react the way the other person wanted you to. Now you know how to choose *your own reactions* in all seven cases—no matter how much power the other person tries to take away from you.

ASK YOURSELF...

1. Think of a time when you saw a man who showed Acted-Out Anger. How manly, versus childish, does he seem to you now? How did you react to him then? What different ways could you react to him now?

2. What's an example of a man showing Irresponsible Anger? How manly, versus childish, does he seem to you now? How did you react to him then? What different ways could you react to him now?

3. When have you seen a man showing Self-Centered Anger? How manly, versus childish, does he seem to you now? How did you react to him then? What different ways could you react to him now?

4. Who have you seen showing Two-Faced Anger? How manly, versus childish, does he seem to you now? How did you react to him then? What different ways could you react to him now?

5. When have you seen a man showing Rigid Anger? How manly, versus childish, does he seem to you now? How did you react to him then? What different ways could you react to him now?

6. Think of a time when you saw a man showing Drinking/Drugging Anger. How manly, versus childish, does he seem to you now? How did you react to him then? What different ways could you react to him now?

7. Who have you seen showing Delusional Anger? How did you react to him then? What different ways could you react to him now?

4

Decide Whether to Talk Now— When You're Angry
Skill #1

Y ou know how to put S-P-A-C-E between what you *feel* and what you *do*. You also know how to stay in charge of *your own* reactions when other people are angry.

Now you'll see how to stay in charge of yourself when *you're* angry. There are seven skills to use. It will take *all seven* before you can really work things out with the other person. No single skill will take care of all of it right away. But each skill plays a part, and each skill is needed.

In this chapter, we'll cover Skill #1: Decide Whether to Talk Now.

The minute you feel angry, make the S-P-A-C-E between that feeling, and *ask yourself* two questions:

1. **Do you want to talk things over with the other person,** *right now*? You may not want to talk things over at all. You may want to *stay* angry at them forever. Or, even if you *do* want to talk things over with them, you may not be ready *right now*. Let's be honest—sometimes, feeling angry can *feel good* for a while, because you feel so righteous and justified to be angry at them.

If you want to stay angry at them forever, do everything you can to just avoid them, so you won't get angry at them anymore.

If you want to talk things over, but *not right now,* not while you feel so righteous and justified—*wait*. Do *not* do anything except remove yourself *until the moment you can answer "yes"* to this question.

The rest of the skills won't work until your answer to Question #1 is "yes."

2. **Even if *you* want to talk things over with this person, do *they* want to talk things over with *you?*** Just because *you're* ready to work on the anger with them *doesn't* necessarily mean *they're* ready! So even when you're ready, you still have to wait until *their* answer is "yes." None of these seven skills will work unless *both* you and the other person can answer "yes" to questions #1 and #2.

Here's something to be careful of. People who get angry in any of the seven ways we talked about earlier may *seem* like they *don't* want to talk things over with you. And that may be true. But the skills described in this book can build on even the *smallest shred* of willingness the other person may have. It helps if you stay open to the chance that they *may* want to work it out with you. It also helps if you start out by *assuming* they want to but they just need your help in using these seven skills.

If you ask them—or you just start using the skills—and nothing works, it's time to give up. We'll talk more about that in Skill #7. For now, we'll assume that both you and he are ready, so you can see how to use all the skills.

When your answers to both questions are "yes," you're ready to use the next six skills to take charge of your own anger. You might not always use all six. And you might use them in a different order. But the first skill is always the same: Deciding if *both* you and the person you're angry at *want* to solve it *now*.

ASK YOURSELF...

1. Think of someone you've been angry at in the last two weeks. Did you want to stay angry, at least for a while? Did you (after a while) want to work it out with them? Did they want to work it out with you?

2. For you personally, what is the hardest thing about wanting to work it out with a person you're angry at? How much does pride get in the way? Wanting to prove something? Having something over him? What do you think you might lose if you talk things over with him?

3. Think of a person you know who "always has to be right." Would he want to talk things over with someone he was mad at? How much like a man—and how much like a child—does he seem to you when he's angry?

5

Talk to the Right Person—When You're Angry
Skill #2

Once you've decided that you both want to talk things over, the next thing to do is use Skill #2: Talk to the Right Person.

What to Do

This isn't as easy as it sounds. For some reason, most persons tell all their friends how angry they are at someone *before* they tell the person they're angry at. It looks like this:

You tell your buddies how angry you are at this person.	Your buddies tell you either to get over it or to go beat him up.	The other person has no idea there's a problem (so he can't work it out with you).
	OR	OR
	They go tell the other person that you're angry and out to get him.	*He* gets angry at you and/or your buddies — and things get worse.

In either case, there is no room for Skill #1—Deciding that you (and he) are ready to fix it. Instead, either the person doesn't know anything about your anger, or the anger increases and the chances of working things out get slimmer. In either case, you've just *given up your power* to both your buddies *and* the person you're angry at! *They* will decide what to do about your anger—when *you* should be the one who decides.

To stay in charge of your own anger, the best thing you can do for yourself is *go directly to the person you're angry at,* and tell him yourself that you're angry. *How* you tell him is going to make all the difference, and we'll talk about that in a few minutes. But for now, the important thing to know is that as soon as you decide that you (and he) are willing to at least talk things over, the best thing you can do for yourself is go tell *him*. It looks like this:

You tell the person (in the way you'll see how to tell him) that you're angry and you want to talk about it with him.	He either is willing to talk it over, or wants to think about it first and talk it over later, or wants to stay angry at you, or couldn't care less. In any case, he knows you're angry at him, and you've given him a chance to talk things over with you.

No matter which of these ways he reacts, *you've* done the best you can to let him know you're angry and to give him a chance to talk it over with you. You've kept it between him and you. You haven't dragged in your buddies or anyone else who's not involved. And you've taken control, and stayed in charge, of *your own* anger. It takes a *real man* to do this.

How to Do It

But talking to the person you're angry at is only part of Skill #2. You *also* have to be in charge of *how* you talk to him. Here's why: *how* you talk is just as important as *what* you say. It looks like this:

You say:	"I'm pissed, and it's *your fault!*"
He reacts:	"Who the hell cares?" or "Oh yeah? It's *your* fault!"

This won't go very far, because *how* you talked to him made him feel defensive, challenged, and pushed into a corner. Also, by making things his "fault," you gave up your power and let him be in charge of your feelings.

OR

You say: "I'm pissed *at you!*"
He reacts: "Oh yeah? Well *I'm* pissed at *you!*"

This time, *how* you talked to him made him feel threatened, as if you think "all" of him is "bad." And your way of talking has not left any room for discussion with him.

Instead, you can say it a different way—a way that doesn't accuse him, doesn't push him into a corner, and doesn't put all the blame on him. For example:

You say: "I'm angry at you *for what you told the boss* about me. "

OR

"I'm pissed because you *still haven't paid me back* the money you owe me."

OR

"I'm pissed because you tried to *hit on my girlfriend*."

In these three examples, you focus on *what he did* that made you angry—his *actions*, instead of "all" of him. And you're being *specific*, instead of having a "general" anger towards him.

Remember that you are not going to fix everything with this skill (or any of the seven skills) *by itself.* But what you *will do* is tell the person about your anger *in a way he's more likely to hear it.* And, in a way that will make him more *willing* to talk it over with you.

The person may deny that he said anything bad to the boss, or come up with excuses about not paying you back, or swear he didn't mean anything about what he said to your girlfriend. *At this point,* neither of you is ready to resolve anything. All you're trying to do, at Skill #2, is go to the person you're angry at, bring up the subject, and start talking it over.

You've started with Skill #1: Decide Whether to Talk Now. You've gotten to Skill #2: Talk to the Right Person (in the right way). The rest of the skills, combined, will help you fix the problem between you and him.

ASK YOURSELF...

1. How often do you tell your buddies before you tell the person you're angry at? What happened when you told your buddies first?

2. Who's the easiest person for you to tell you're angry at them? Who's the hardest person for you to say it to?

3. What's the hardest thing about telling the person you're angry at? The easiest?

4. What are some good results that came from how you said you were angry? What are examples of bad results that came from how you said it?

6

Pay Attention To Their Feelings—
When You're Angry
Skill #3

Y ou've used Skill #1: Decide Whether to Talk Now. You've done Skill #2: Talk to the Right Person. Now you're ready for Skill #3: Pay Attention to *Their* Feelings. This *isn't* a touchy-feely thing. This is a tactical move, like in football or business, to stay in charge of your anger.

Let's start with what happens if you *don't* pay attention to their feelings. This is typical:

You're angry at a person.

You tell him you're *angry*, why it's *his* fault, how *right* you are about it, and how *he's* to blame not only for *this* problem, but other problems *also*.	He gets defensive, refuses to listen, says "Oh, yeah?" and starts to prove how it's all *your* fault. And, he gets really angry at *you*.

The result is that *both* of you end up angry, nothing gets settled, and the two of you don't get along anymore. Is this all familiar to you?

But if you pay attention to *his* feelings *also*, there's a good chance that two very different things will happen. First, he will feel as if he, as a person and as a man, *matters*. He *counts*. You're *not* treating him like a piece of dirt or an object that's in the way. Feeling like he *matters* as a person will make him less defensive, less threatened, and less likely to think you want to "win" at his "expense." He'll be more likely to listen.

46

Second, if you pay attention to his feelings, his anger will go _down_. Not low enough to "solve" everything right then. But low enough for him to _talk_ with you about _your_ anger. And that's your goal—getting him to talk it over with you. It looks like this:

You're angry at a person.

You tell him you're angry, _and that you can tell HE's_ angry, annoyed, upset, or _whatever_ you think he feels at the time. Then you tell you want to talk things over with him.

He feels like he _counts_ as a man. He is less defensive and more willing to hear about _your_ anger and more willing to talk things over with you.

In Skill #1, you decided you both were willing to talk. In Skill #2, you went to the person you're angry at. In Skill #3, you pay attention to _their_ feelings, as well as your own. Once you pay attention to their feelings, and they're more willing to listen and talk, _how_ you talk with them will be important again.

More About _What_ You Say and _How_ You Say It

Try this: Frown, scowl, and look as _negative_ and _critical_ as you can. Then, say, "I'm so _happy!_"

Try another exercise: Smile, lift your eyebrows, and raise your eyes up. Then, say, "I'm so _down!_"

Now stand up, cross your arms in front of you, tap one foot quickly on the floor, make the corners of your mouth point down, and frown. Then, say, "I'm a very patient man. You can come talk to me anytime."

Hard to do? Does it feel strange? Out of sync? Torn in different directions? In all three cases, _what_ you say doesn't match _how_ you say it. It feels strange because you're giving _two very different messages_ at the same time. In the first case, your face says you're negative and sour, but your words say you're happy. In the second case, your face says you're happy but your words say you're sad. In the third case, you body says you're closed, impatient, and unapproachable, but your words say you're patient and open.

So far, there are two things to get from these examples:

1. **People will believe you *only* when *what* you say matches *how* you say it.** When your *what* and *how* contradict each other, people feel nervous around you.

2. **If your *what* and *how* don't match, people will believe your *how* no matter *what* you say.** In the first case, they'll believe you're critical and negative because of *how* you say it, and they *won't* believe you're "happy" even though that's *what* you say. In the second case, they'll believe you're *happy* because that's *how* you say it, and they won't believe *what* you say. In the third case, they'll believe you're impatient and closed, because of *how* you say it—regardless of *what* you say.

These two points show you that *how* you talk is just as important as *what* you say.

When you're angry, paying attention to *both*—*what* and *how*—keeps you in charge of your anger. First, let's look again at the typical way it goes when you don't pay attention to the other person's feelings:

You're angry at a person.

You tell him you're *angry*, why it's *his* fault, how *right* you are about it, and how *he's* to blame not only for *this* problem, but other problems *also*.	He gets defensive, refuses to listen, says "Oh, yeah?" and starts to prove how it's all *your* fault. And, he gets really angry at *you*.

Your *what* is negative and critical—telling him it's his fault, that you're right, and how he's to blame for lots of problems. The odds are that *how* you say it—your face, body language, and tone of voice—also are negative and critical. Because both your *what* and *how* are the same, the person believes that you mean what you say—that you're right, he's wrong, and it's all his fault. No wonder he gets defensive!

And, going a step further: when *how* you come across about *your* feelings is so strong, it sounds to the other person as if *only you* are going to get what you want from this conversation. When your *how* is so strong about *only you,* there's no room for *him* or *his* feelings. What's in it *for him* to try to work things out with you?

It's a different story when you let him know that he counts also. Let's look again at what happens when you pay attention to *his* feelings:

You're angry at a person.

You tell him you're angry, *and that you can tell HE's* angry, annoyed, upset, or *whatever* you think he feels at the time. Then you tell him you want to talk things over with him.

He feels like he *counts* as a man He is less defensive and more willing to hear about *your* anger.

This time, your *what* includes you *and* him. You're angry *and* you know that he has feelings as well. It's not just about you. And the odds are that your *how* matches what you say—straightforward, open, willing to listen as well as talk. Because your *how* matches your *what,* he believes you mean what you say—that you're angry, you know *he* has his own feelings also, and that you want to talk *with* (not against) him.

This time, your *how* has room for both of you. You want to talk things over for *both* of your sakes. That's why he's more likely to be willing to talk and work things out with you.

And back to *you.* By paying attention to both your *what* and *how,* you keep *yourself* in charge of your anger. You don't let your anger go off by itself, and you don't let the other person shut you and your anger out.

At Skill #1, you decided you and he were willing to try to work things out. At Skill #2, you went to the person you're angry at. And at Skill #3, you keep things going by paying attention to *his* feelings, as well as your own.

And *you're* staying in charge of your anger.

ASK YOURSELF...

1. Which of these feelings do men let themselves feel: angry, loving, jealous, happy, brave, afraid?

2. What feelings do most men admit they feel?

3. What feelings might most men not admit to? Why won't they admit experiencing them?

4. What feelings are the hardest for men to talk about with each other?

5. What happens to men who can't, or don't, talk to anyone about their feelings?

Checklist

1. Look at the list below.

2. For each item, notice *all* the feelings you might have at the same time.

3. Notice *which feelings* are okay for you, and *which feelings* make you uncomfortable.

- ❏ Guns
- ❏ Babies
- ❏ Bars
- ❏ Women
- ❏ Outdoors/nature
- ❏ Police
- ❏ Family
- ❏ Blood
- ❏ Wife
- ❏ War
- ❏ Significant other
- ❏ Child abusers
- ❏ War
- ❏ Hospitals
- ❏ Girlfriend
- ❏ Prisons
- ❏ Drugs
- ❏ Church
- ❏ Your face
- ❏ Your child/children
- ❏ Divorce
- ❏ Your work
- ❏ Money

7

Find Something In Common— When You're Angry
Skill #4

You've done Skill #1, deciding you're both willing to work things out. You've done Skill #2, going to the person you're angry at. You did Skill #3, paying attention to the other person's feelings. And now you're ready for Skill #4: Find Something in Common with the person you're angry at.

You are not ready to find something in common until you've done the first three skills. This is because without the first three, you and the other person would have either gotten into a fight, ignored each other, or dropped it after an uneasy start. The first three skills have gotten you to a place where you, and he, can start to talk things over.

But—Skill #4 isn't going to "solve everything" yet either. Skill #4, Find Something in Common, is going to help you and the other person work together better on it. You're still building towards working things out. And you're staying in charge of your anger.

Finding something in common is important because it lets each of you get something for yourself out of talking and working things out. When there's something in it for both of you, you're both more likely to hang in there and work on it.

You can think in advance about what you have in common with people you sometimes get angry at. The relationship might be what you have in common—your marriage, your friendship, the fact that you work in the same building with each other every day. The activities might be what you have in common—hunting with a few of your buddies, boating with others. What you and a co-worker might have in common is the need to look good to your boss. The point is to find something in common that makes *both* of you willing to keep working on the anger problem.

Let's look again at the conversation when you pay attention to the other person's feelings, and move toward finding something in common.

You're angry at a person.

You tell him you're angry, and that you can tell HE's angry, annoyed, upset, or whatever you think he feels at the time. Then you tell him you want to talk things over with him.

He feels like he counts as a man. He is less defensive and more willing to hear about your anger and more willing to talk things over with you.

Now that you've paid attention to his feelings, and he's willing to hear your side and talk things over with you, the next thing you can do is tell him what you both have in common. Your part of the conversation could go something like these examples:

You pay attention to his feelings:

"I'm angry about something you did. I can see that you're pretty pissed yourself right now. Let's talk it over."

After he agrees, you find something in common:

"Good. We're friends. We've got to work this out."

OR

"Good. We both want to the boss to see that we're getting along."

Or whatever else fits the situation. What you find in common helps "cement" the decision for *both* of you to keep working at it.

Skill #1 got you to decide that both of you were willing to talk. Skill #2 got you talking to the person you're angry at. Skill #3 got you to pay attention to his feelings, as well as yours. Skill #4 helps you find something in common, so you're both motivated.

And you're still in control of your own anger.

ASK YOURSELF...

1. Who are three people you often get angry at?

2. What do you have in common with each of them?

8

Depersonalize the Situation—
When You're Angry
Skill #5

You've used four skills so far: deciding both you and he are willing to talk, going to the person you're angry at, paying attention to his feelings (as well as yours), and finding something in common. Now you're ready for Skill #5: Depersonalize the Situation—which means *don't* take things personally.

It's easy to take things personally. Especially when you're angry. But when you take things personally, three things work *against* you:

- **You feel as if *you*, the whole person, are being judged as "bad."** The truth is, what's being judged is *something you did—not* all of who you are.

- **You get defensive, so you can't listen.** As you know, working things out with the other person means you'll have to listen to what he says. If you take things personally, your defensiveness will stop you from listening.

- **You can't work things out with the other person.** To talk about your anger and his feelings, you have to be able to talk! When you take things personally, you've lost control of your ability to talk calmly enough to resolve anything.

If you take things *personally*, you're letting yourself act like a *child*, not a *man*. You're not putting any S-P-A-C-E between what you *feel* and what you *do*. That S-P-A-C-E—and the *thinking* you do in that S-P-A-C-E— make all the difference.

How to *Not* Take Things Personally

1. **Remind yourself that it's not about *all* of you.** If someone's mad at you, he's mad about something you *said* or *did*. He's not angry at the whole person you are. He's not angry at your life, your birth, your history, your smarts, your strengths, and the billions of other things that make you who you are. Remind yourself that his anger is *limited* to *specific things,* not *you.*

2. **Ask yourself, "How much is his anger about what *I* did or said, and how much of his anger is about *him*?"** What you did or said may have hurt him in some ways. You have to be honest with yourself, and accept that he may have a right to be angry. You still may think you did or said the right thing, or that he deserved it—but here you have to look at it from *his* point of view.

   Then, you have to ask yourself how much of his anger is about *him.* Some people go through life angry most of the time, and they look for other people to take it out on. Ask yourself how much of their anger is justified, or at least understandable, and how much of it really is about him.

3. **Ask yourself if what you *think* is going on really *is* going on.** You may have heard *rumors* about him being angry at you. You may have heard *part* of what he said, and filled in the rest—*incorrectly*—in your own mind. You may be *wrong* about thinking he's mad at you. Or, if he *is* angry, you may have the wrong idea about *why,* or *how much.* Before jumping to conclusions and making assumptions, get out of *your personal* mindset and find out where *he's* really at.

   And, before we get into how to talk to the other person in a depersonalized way, there is one more key item:

4. ***Do not MAKE* it personal!** It works against you if you *take* things personally, and it also works against you if you *make* it personal for the other person. Use the steps in the next section, to talk to him in a *depersonalized* way.

How to Talk in a Depersonalized Way

You've used the first four skills already: decided you both were willing to talk, went to the person you're angry at, paid attention to his feelings (as well as your own), and found something in common. Now you're ready to talk to him *about your anger* in a *depersonalized* way.

Here are the steps to follow:

1. ***Own* your anger.** Do *not* say, "*You made* me angry!"—because that gives *him* power over you. You're saying that *he* controls *your* anger. Instead, say, "*I'm* angry at you!"—because that keeps *you* in charge of your anger. To be in charge of your own anger, *you* have to *own* it.

2. **Talk about his *actions* or *words, NOT* about *him.*** Do *NOT* say,

   "*You're* an asshole! *You* don't know what you're doing!" It's not *him,* the whole person, you're angry at. You're angry at something he *did* or *said.* So instead, tell him, "I'm angry at you *calling me stupid!*" or "I'm pissed off at you for *hitting on my girlfriend!*" or "I'm angry at you for *telling the boss I lied.*"

   When you talk about being angry at what he *did* or *said,* that's a lot *less* personal than saying you're angry at *him.* It also gives you both room to talk about *why* he did or said it, what *you* could do or say differently to him, how *he* could act or talk differently to you or about you. It gives both of you room to change things for the better—by learning about yourselves and each other.

3. **Find out what's *behind* his actions or words.** Do *NOT* assume anything! It will make you sound like you're *accusing* him, and things will get worse instead of better. For example: do *not* say, "I'm angry at you calling me stupid. *You trying to make me look bad?*"

   Instead, *ask* why he did what he did or said what he said. And be careful of *HOW* you ask. Make sure it doesn't sound like an accusation, like "You trying to make me look bad?" sounds.

   Say: "I'm angry at you calling me stupid. *Why did you say that?*" Or, "I'm angry at you for hitting on my girlfriend. What's going on?" Or, "I'm angry at you telling the boss I lied. What did you do that for?"

   By *asking*—instead of assuming or accusing—you are more likely to learn something.

After you've asked why he acted or spoke the way he did, a lot depends on the reasons he gives you. Maybe he was getting even with you for something *you* did or said. Maybe he was joking—or thought he was, or wants *you* to think he was. Maybe he had no idea what he was saying or doing at the time. And maybe you misinterpreted him—or maybe what you thought (or heard) happened *didn't* happen. A lot depends on what you find out here.

If he was getting even with you for something, you can make a deal with him—you'll stop (or change) if he does. If he was joking, you need to tell him (in a way described below) that you would like him to stop those kinds of jokes. If he was blind to what he did or said, you can ask him (in a way described below) to be more careful when he talks about you. If you misinterpreted him—or if the event didn't even happen—you can apologize (in a way described below) and thank him for talking about it with you.

4. **Talk about** *specific changes* **you want.** Do *NOT* be vague, general—or personal. If you want him to change his behavior or words, *don't* say he should "show more respect" or "watch" what he says. These ways of talking are too general and too easy to interpret in different ways. What *he* calls "respect" or "watching" what he says may be very different from what *you want.*

Instead of being too general, get *very* specific. For example: "I'm angry at you calling me stupid. Why did you say that?" If he says he was joking, a specific, depersonalized way to ask for the change you want is: "Don't make jokes like that about me anymore."

This is much more specific than "Watch what you say." It's also much less accusatory, and much less personal. You can't control whether he changes his behavior or not. But you've given him a chance by speaking up, and you can decide whether or how to deal with him, depending on what he does.

If you say, "I'm angry at you for hitting on my girlfriend. What's going on?" his answer might be that he "must have been drunk."

Whether you believe him or not, a specific and depersonalized way to ask for the change you want is to say something like, "Please pay more attention to what you're doing." You can't control his actions, but you've let him know that you're aware of his actions.

You can decide later whether or how to relate to him, depending on what he does.

If you tell him, "I'm angry at you telling the boss I lied. What did you do that for?," he may say, "Well, you *did* lie. You called in sick, but you really weren't." You can ask for the change you want by saying something like, "I'd like you to keep what you know about my personal life separate from work." Again, you can't control his actions. But you can make him aware of what you want. You also can decide how close a friend you want to be, depending on what he does after you've asked for a change.

Depersonalizing makes it possible for you and the other person to talk about the things that make you angry—and about changes that can help.

You've used Skill #1, deciding that both of you are willing to talk. With Skill #2, you went directly to the person you're angry at. In Skill #3, you paid attention to his feelings (as well as your own). In Skill #4, you found something in common between the two of you. And in Skill #5, you've started talking about your anger in depersonalized ways.

ASK YOURSELF...

1. What are examples of people you know "pushing your buttons"—making personal comments that they know will "get you" angry?

2. How do you usually react when they do this?

3. How does your usual reaction make you feel?

4. What could you say that would depersonalize these situations?

9

Get to the Real Issue(s)—When You're Angry
Skill #6

The first five skills got you—and the other person—ready to get to the *real issue*. You decided that both of you were willing to talk, you went to the person you're angry at, you paid attention to his feelings (as well as your own), you found something in common, and you depersonalized the anger. All these skills have to be done before you (or he) can use Skill #6: Get to the *Real* Issue(s) about your anger (and his).

First, let's take a look at what the ***real*** issue means.

The *Real* Issue

When you're angry, it happens on two different levels. The first level is all the *details* that you're angry about. For example: a person cut you off on the freeway, someone called you a nasty name, you didn't get the raise you deserve, your wife keeps nagging you, you can't afford the car you want, someone didn't do what you said, your buddy didn't return the money you loaned him. All these facts are the *details* that you're angry about.

But it goes deeper than that. The second level is what the details *mean* to you, what the details *say about* you, and what the other person *thinks* of you. The second level is what the details *mean* to you, about *you.*

Here are examples of how the first level—the *details*—relates to the second level—what the details *mean* to you, *about* you:

Details	Possible meaning *to you–about you*
Someone cuts you off on the freeway.	You're *nobody.*
	He thinks you're nobody.
	You're *less of a man* than he is.

60

Someone called you a nasty name.	You're *second-class.* You're *less of a man* than he is. *He* thinks you're dirt.
You didn't get the raise you deserve.	You're not good enough. You're stupid. You don't really deserve the raise. *Your boss* thinks you're nobody. You're *less of a man* than he is.
Your wife keeps nagging you.	You're *not a real man.*
You can't afford the car.	You're *worthless*—just like your car. You're *not a real man.*
Someone didn't do what you said.	You have *no* control, *no* power. You're *less of a man* than he is.
Your buddy didn't return the money you loaned him.	You're a *mark.* You're a *sucker.* You're *less of man* than he is.

The first level—the *details*—catch your attention. But the second level—what the details *mean* to you, *about you*—is where your anger comes from.

Another way to look at the two levels:

Details = Symptoms (like a sore throat or a cough)
What the Details *Mean* to You, *About You* = Real Issue (like
strep throat or a cold)

A sore throat or cough tells you something's wrong, but they are only the *symptoms.* You can't really cure or "fix" them until you know the *real issue*—is it strep throat, or only a cold?

In the same way, the *details*—the person cutting you off on the freeway, not getting the raise—are the *symptoms* that you notice. But the *meaning about you*—that you're worthless, that you're less of a man—are the *real issues* that trigger your anger.

To get to the heart of your anger, and to resolve it, you have to talk about the *real issue,* not the symptoms.

How to Talk About the Real Issue

If you talk only about the *symptoms,* you'll never get to the *real issue.* Instead, you and the other person will go round and round over the details (symptoms), and things will get worse. Here's an example:

You:	"Do you know when you'll pay me back the money you borrowed?
Other Person:	"Yeah, well, soon. What's the big deal?"
You:	"What do you mean, 'what's the big deal'? Last time you borrowed from me, it took almost a year before you paid it back. This time, you said you'd pay in two weeks. It's been three months."
Other Person:	"It wasn't a year, it was eight months. I said I'd pay you back as soon as I got my overtime check. It should have been here by now, but I still don't have it."
You:	"Well, if you'd follow up at work, maybe you'd get your check sooner. You just let things slide, and that's why things are never on time."
Other Person:	"Look who's talking! Remember the money I loaned you to fix your old car, and it wasn't till you sold the damn thing that you paid me back!"
You:	"The only reason that car had to be fixed is that I loaned it to *you,* and you *wrecked* it! You should have paid for the damn repairs in the first place!"
Other Person:	"Oh, yeah? Well......"

Is this familiar? Do you see how many other issues are getting brought into the conversation? How close are you to getting your money back? This conversation will keep getting worse, as more and more *details*—symptoms—are brought into it. In this type of conversation, you might lose your money *and* your friend.

To get to the *real issue,* you have to get past the symptoms.

You:	"Do you know when you'll pay me back the money you borrowed?"
Other Person:	"Yeah, well, soon. What's the big deal?"
You:	"The big deal isn't the money. I feel taken advantage of when you're slow to pay it back."
Other Person:	"You mean, like I'm stealing it?"
You:	"No. It's like I don't count. When you take your time paying it back, it feels like you don't think I'm important."

You can't control his reaction. But you've left out all the details (symptoms), and you've told him what his slow repayment *means* to you (the real issue). He may say, "Oh, sure, no problem. I'll pay you back tomorrow." He may say, "I never thought of it that way." He may be silent because no one's ever gotten to the real issue so easily before.

Here's another example of talking about the real issue:

Your wife:	"You still haven't taken care of the yard, and my car is still making that noise. Why do you take so long to take care of things?"
You:	(Instead of arguing about whose fault it is, or how many other things you've taken care of, or dragging in a bunch of symptoms that will just make things worse.) "It sounds like you think I've been letting you down a lot lately about getting chores done. Is that what I seem to be doing?"

Your wife may say, "Yes, that's exactly how I see it." Or she may say, "You know, it isn't you at all. I've just been so busy that things are getting on my nerves." You can't control her reaction. But by getting to the real issue, you give both of you a chance to talk things over. And sometimes, by getting to *your* real issue, you help the other person get to *theirs.*

When you get to the other person's real issue also, it's easier for *both* of you to talk about what bothers you and what you want from each other. One of the things you may find out is that sometimes *your real issue—* what their words or actions *meant to you* about *you—is not* what they meant to say about you. They may even be surprised to hear how you took what they said. How you took it, and how that felt to you, are *real*. But the source may have been their *blindness*, not their ill will. Your friend may not have realized that returning the money late made you feel unimportant. Your wife may not have realized that she was taking her own problems out on you. Getting to the real issue helps you find this out. It helps resolve your anger.

However, there *are* times when the other person *meant* it in the way you took it. In these cases, your *real issue* changes.

Sometimes the Real Issue Changes

In the examples so far, you and the other person are able to resolve things because of Skill #1: You *both* want to work on the issues. But there also are times when the other person does *not* want to work things out with you. They may purposely *want* to put you down, and it's not a misunderstanding at all.

In these cases, you have *two* real issues:

(1) The meaning *to* you, *about* you, of his words or actions.

(2) The fact that he does *not* want to work things out with you and, instead, he said what he said, or did what he did, because he *wants* you to feel bad.

If you get even with him, yell in his face, call him names back, hit him, or react in *any* way that shows you're angry, guess who wins? He *got* you, his nasty words or actions *got* to you, he has *power* over you. *He* feels like a *real man* because he *got* you! Do you want to give him that?

The hard part is that all these reactions would be natural, because of your *first* real issue: the *meaning* of his words or actions are that you are *nothing* and you *don't matter*—so of course you feel angry. It's hard enough to put a S-P-A-C-E between what you *feel* and what you *do* when you're angry.

But even harder, your *second* real issue makes it much worse—you got the point that he *wants* you to feel bad, and that makes you even angrier. His doing it *on purpose* gives your anger a double whammy.

Most men can't hold back on the second real issue, even if they can hold back on the first. This means that even if most men *could* stay in charge of their own anger when they feel put down, they *can't* stay in charge when they know the put-down was *on purpose.* They feel trapped in a corner, and they start fighting their way out. They lose control of themselves.

And as soon as you lose control of your anger because of the *second* real issue, you let the person who wants to put you down take charge of *your* anger.

Here's how to get out of this trap:

1. ***Do NOT try to talk or reason with this person.*** When you *know* that his goal is to make you feel bad, Skill #1 cannot take place. So none of the other skills will work with him.

2. ***Let yourself feel the anger you feel.*** It's real, you know the source, and it's okay to *feel* it.

3. ***Make a S-P-A-C-E between your anger and your actions.*** In this S-P-A-C-E , tell yourself that your *first* real issue—feeling bad because of what this person is saying or doing—has to give way right now to your *second* real issue—the fact that he's doing it on purpose, and you want to stay *in charge* of your own anger.

When you give yourself the S-P-A-C-E to focus on the second real issue, you want to decide what you could do or say that will take away his power. Remember that he wants to be able to *get* to you. So what can *you* do or say that looks like he *didn't* make you feel bad?

One way might be to ignore him. Another might be to smile and nod your head in a friendly way. Another might be to shake his hand and say, "I'm glad you can be honest about how you feel." There is no "magic" way that will always work. *You* have to decide what you can do or say that will make you look *unaffected* by his words or actions. *Un-"got"* by them.

And your next goal is to *get away* from him. When his goal is to put you down and "get" you, hanging around with him will only make things worse for you.

When you have to take all these steps for the second real issue, you still will have your angry feelings to deal with—*later,* when you're away from him, and he won't know. In the next chapter, we talk about how to deal with your anger *later.*

One more thing: sometimes, when you're dealing with a person who does *not* want to work things out with you and you have to deal with the second real issue, you may have to get some *authority* behind you. For example: If you're being attacked (by words or fists), you need to get the police. If you're being called names on the job, your boss or Human Resource person can help, because harassment in the workplace is illegal. If you're being hassled by another prisoner at work, the help you need may be *official* (from the psychologist, guard, or warden) or *unofficial* (from the prisoners who *really* run things).

After You've Discussed the Real Issue

In situations where the other person *does* want to work things out with you, there is one more step to take after you've talked about the real issue: You and the other person have to decide what each of you will *do*, based on your discussion. For example, he may agree to pay you back sooner from now on. You may agree to be more specific about when you need the money back.

Once you decide what each of you will do, you then have to *do* it. If you don't, there's likely to be another round of anger later on.

In all these situations and examples, you've done Skill #6, Get to the *Real* Issue(s). This is where issues get solved and anger gets resolved.

ASK YOURSELF...

1. What are three things people do or say that make you angry? (These are the details, or the symptoms.)

2. For each one: what meanings about you (the real issues) do you get from these examples?

3. In what ways might you be uncomfortable talking about the real issues with someone you're angry at?

4. In what ways might you be comfortable talking about the real issues with someone you're angry at?

10

Drop the Grudge—When You're Angry
Skill #7

Y ou've decided both of you were willing to talk, you went to the
person you're angry at, you paid attention to the other person's
feelings (as well as your own), you found something in common,
you depersonalized how you talked about it, and you got to the real issues
(and did what you agreed to do). It sounds like you're done with your anger
skills—but we still have Skill #7: Drop the Grudge. This is harder—and
more important—than you think.

There are *three parts* to dropping the grudge. The first part comes
right after you and the other person got to the real issues and agreed about
what each of you would do — but *before* you come through with what you
said *you'd* do.

Here's why: if you *don't* drop the grudge against this person, you
won't do what you agreed to do. Or, you'll do it in a half-hearted or *grudg-
ing* way. And the anger between the two of you will come back—worse
than before. To stay in charge of your anger, you have to *let go* of grudges.

Letting go is hard—especially of grudges. Once again, you have to
face the fact that *either* you *or* your anger is going to be in charge. Holding
onto the grudge might feel justified. It probably feels *good*. But it gives all
your power to your *anger*, instead of your*self*. Here's how to let go of your
grudge in order to do what you agreed to do:

How to Drop the Grudge So You Can Act Now

1. **Remember to *depersonalize*.** What he did wasn't about you—it
    was about *him*.

2. **You've already had your say.** He already knows how you felt, and you know how he felt. You don't have to hash over the same stuff again.

3. **You have something to gain.** You're *not* "giving in" or "giving up" when you do what you said you'd do. You're doing your part of fixing the problem and working things out with him.

4. **You have nothing to lose.** You're doing the right thing by doing your part. If he doesn't do his part, you didn't "lose" anything or become a "sucker." *He* did—because he lost control of his anger and let it boss him around.

If you keep these things in mind, it's easier for you to do the *first part* of dropping the grudge—and to do what you agreed to do. When you do your part, you help fix the anger between you and the other person. And you stay in charge of *your* anger.

The *second part* of dropping the grudge is more long-term. It can apply to one person, but it also applies to the general ways you deal with your anger and hold grudges.

Holding grudges can give you something to *hold onto.* They are a very *macho* thing to have. But the bad part is, they keep you *angry.* You're *not* "wrong" to feel this way. But it works against you. The longer you hold onto grudges and anger, the more *they* take control of *you.* That's why you have to let go of them—so *you* can be in charge.

Letting Go of Grudges in General

Letting go is hard. Let's look at the steps and see what's hard about each step.

Step 1: Denial. Denial means you *can't see* how the grudges you hold are controlling you. Even if you "know," in your mind, that they control you, it's hard to *believe* it in your guts. Why? Because it's not manly to let something *control you.* So you have a hard time admitting that's what's happening.

Step 2: Giving them up. Like alcohol, drugs, gambling, smoking, workaholism, or a lot of other things that aren't good for you, grudges are hard to give up. They make you feel righteous, justified, like a winner. They make you feel like a man.

But they have their "morning after," too. They take over your thoughts. They make you focus on the negative. They take a lot of your time. They cost you your health and your money. They take away your energy. They can make you lose your job, your friends, your family. They block out the good things—including people—in your life.

And like other addictions, *they take charge of your life.* Like all addictions, your grudges, and the people you have grudges against, *control you.* How manly is *that?*

Giving up your grudges leaves a big hole in your life *–for a while.* That's why most addicts can't quit for long. It takes a *real man* to give up what's destroying him.

Step 3: Healing. While you're giving up the grudges, the most *painful* part—the part that makes quitting so hard for addicts—is the fact that *healing hurts.*

Think of a time you cut your hand. The second the cut happens, you don't feel anything—you're in shock, you're numb, you don't feel any pain. But as soon as the cut starts to *heal,* it hurts like hell.

It's the same for healing *emotionally,* in your *guts.* The hole in your life is what hurts when the grudge starts to leave. The loneliness, the feelings of being left out, the fears everyone has but men don't talk about. Like any addiction, holding grudges fills the hole *for a while.* But they're only short-term fillings. It takes more and more of them to keep that hole filled. The only way to *really* fill that hole in your guts is something we'll talk about later, in Step 4. But grudges, like other addictions, *don't* do it. So you keep getting more and more things to be angry about, more and more people to get angry at, to fill that hole. And when you quit the short-term filler, that hole opens up again and you hurt.

You'll hurt in different ways. You'll try to *hide* all these hurts, because they don't fit the "manly" stereotype. But you'll go through the same things as the heroin or coke addict having physical (and emotional) withdrawal. Here's what you'll feel *inside,* whether you'll admit it to anyone else or not:

- A lot of **anger**—even more anger than you thought you had. You'll want to *show* more anger, in worse ways. And you'll get angry *more easily* than you did before. You'll get angry over *small* things, not just big ones.

- *Fear.* You'll get afraid of things you didn't know you were afraid of. You'll fear small things that don't bother anyone else. You'll fear things that aren't happening. You'll feel afraid in a general way. You'll have trouble knowing what specific things are making you feel afraid.

- **Sadness**. You'll feel sad about things from the past. Feeling happy will make you feel sad. You'll feel sad for no reasons at all. You'll feel sad at times when nothing around you is making you feel that way.

- **Guilt**. You'll feel guilty because of what you did in the past. You'll feel guilty because of what you didn't do. You'll feel guilty when you have a good time. You'll feel guilty when you're sad.

- **Depression**. This is different from sadness. *Sadness* means you feel down, you know it, and (if you can admit it to yourself) you feel like crying. But *depression* means you *don't feel anything*. You may be shocked to learn that anger was the *only* feeling you let yourself have. Your depression may make you feel like jumping into the hole you feel inside.

Healing *hurts* in these ways. That's why it's so hard to go through the healing step, and to give up the grudges in the first place. That's why *many* men, like most addicts, *can't quit*. It takes a *true man* to give up the grudges and go through the healing process.

When all these feelings arise in you, the way to *heal* is to:

- Do *NOT* deny your feelings, ignore them, talk yourself out of them, or "do something" about them. *Just feel them*. Give yourself the time and S-P-A-C-E to feel them.

- Let yourself *feel* everything that you feel. Different feelings will come and go *if you let them*. If you *don't* let them, they'll come anyway, but they'll stay *locked up inside you*—which is what caused all your anger and grudges in the first place. If you let them come, feel them, and let them go, you will heal. *You will get over them without denying them or letting them build up.*

It's typical to pretend you have no feelings and allow yourself to feel only anger. But a *real man* lets himself heal from his anger and grudges.

Step 4: Taking back control of your life. This is your payoff. After you get past your denial, give up your grudges, feel the hole inside, and let yourself heal, you're ready to fill that hole with positive things *you* choose, that are *good* for you. When you take back control of your *anger*, you're ready to take back control of your own *life*. *That's* manly.

The *first part* of dropping your grudge is to be able to do what you agreed to do. The *second part* of letting go is dropping grudges in general—and healing. The *third part* of dropping the grudge is when your *second* real issue is that the other person *doesn't* want to work things out with you.

In Chapter 9, we talked about the person who *purposely* wants to put you down and make you feel bad. You saw how to avoid talking with him, how to feel your own feelings, and how to make a S-P-A-C-E between what you feel and what you do. You saw how to show him that you're *ungot*—and leave. Now you're ready to see—in the next section, "How to Drop the Grudge When the Other Person Wants to *Get* You"— how to deal with your anger *later,* when you're away from him.

How to Drop the Grudge When the Other Person Wants to Get You

When the other person *doesn't* want to work things out with you, and wants to *get* you by putting you down, you have to show that he *didn't* get to you—and then leave. That's the end of having to put up with him.

But it's *not* the end of dealing with your anger. If you just blow it off, it will just build up. After a while, you'll be holding grudges—and losing more and more control of your anger *and* your life. So you *have to* deal with your anger after you get away from the person who's out to *get* you.

Step 1: Admit you're angry. Most men pretend they're not angry about these guys. That's why these sad individuals hold grudges—and let anger control their lives.

Instead, admit *to yourself* that you're angry (and maybe even *hurt)* because of the other person trying to put you down. Remember that you have to know how you *feel* so you can take steps to deal with it.

Step 2: Depersonalize. What he said—and his need to put you down—tell you more about *him* than about *you.* You were the scapegoat for all his problems, but his problems are about *him—not you.* This is *very* different from a person you trust trying to give you some advice.

Step 3: Let yourself heal. You know you felt angry. You also may have felt defensive, fearful, guilty, or other emotions.

■ Do *not* deny or act on your feelings. Just feel them.

■ Let yourself *feel* what you feel. Let the feelings come—and go.

■ Give yourself the time and S-P-A-C-E to do this.

Step 4: Get back to your life. The other person was a nuisance. A bump in the road. Don't give him any more time or energy now. Focus on your own life, activities, and people. Something unexpected may happen: by the time you get back to your life, you may end up *feeling sorry* for the other person. But even if you don't, you're no longer giving him power by staying angry at him. *You're* back in charge.

Grieving

Sometimes, you may be angry because of something much bigger than a grudge. You may be *grieving* the loss of someone, or something, you love. This might come from the death of someone you love, or the loss of a good job, or the loss of your youth—anything that means a *lot* to you. You might grieve over the fact that you can't change things you think are unfair. Or that you can't control situations—or people—you want to control.

Here's how grieving relates to anger. The grieving steps are the *same* as the four steps of "Letting Go of Grudges in General," in the section above. You could call grieving "Letting Go of Someone or Something You Love." When you lose someone or something, you go through all the same steps—with one difference.

The difference is: before you go through Denial—which is Step 1 under "Letting Go of Grudges in General"—the first step in grieving is *Shock*. Shock means you can neither *think* nor *feel*. Both your *mind* and your *guts* are *numb*. Once the reality sinks in, you get out of Shock and go into Denial—and follow all the other steps in "Letting Go of Grudges in General."

Here's a real example of how grieving can affect you in the early stages:

> My police buddy was killed in a helicopter crash. In preparation for his funeral, I took special pains to make sure my brass was polished to perfection, my leather was immaculate, my gun shined and oiled, and my shoes polished to a black mirror. I loaded my thing into my car, and went to headquarters to change for the funeral. As soon as I began dressing, I found that I had forgotten to bring my uniform trousers. I didn't attend the funeral.

If you don't grieve, you stay *stuck*—and *angry*—in the same way you would if you don't let go of grudges. Grieving lets you *feel and then get past* your losses, so you can reach Step 4: Taking back control of your life.

In Skill #1, you decided both you and the other person were willing to talk things over. In Skill #2, you went to the person you're angry at. In Skill #3, you paid attention to his feelings (as well as your own). In Skill #4, you found something in common with him. In Skill #5, you depersonalized. In Skill #6, you got to the real issues. In Skill #7, you let go of your grudge—in the short term, the long term, and in cases where the other person would not cooperate.

These seven skills help you take charge of your anger. *That* takes a *real* man.

Next, we'll take a different look at the stories at the beginning of the book. This time, we'll see how to deal with the same situations *using the seven skills*—the *manly* way to deal with them.

ASK YOURSELF...

1. Think of one person you like holding a grudge against.

2. What do you like about holding this grudge?

3. What would it "cost" you—that is, what would you lose—by letting go of this grudge?

4. How aware are you of the "hole" that the grudge helps "fill"?

5. What other ways do you try to "fill" the "hole"?

6. What might you gain by letting go of this grudge?

11

Applying the Seven Skills to Our Opening Stories

Now, we'll look again at the case stories we started with. You'll see how to use the skills in each story. Each story has its own section:

Jealousy and injustice

When I was in Korea, an Army Captain was in love with a Korean girl who was a whore. She worked at a place the soldiers called Hooker Hill. Apparently he had told himself, "She's not that kind of hooker."

One night, after getting drunk, he went to visit her at work. He walked in and saw her sitting on another guy's lap. The guy's hand was up the skirt of his "girlfriend." The Captain grabbed her by the arm and dragged her outside and down the street. He was dragging her violently, and at one point had her in a headlock.

This was all in plain view of both Korean and U.S. Army police. (Yes, the MPs watched soldiers enter and leave known brothels on a daily basis—the restrictions were never enforced.)

The MPs approached the officer and told him he had to stop what he was doing or he'd be arrested.

"You can't talk to me like that!" he shouted. "I'm a Captain in the ___ MP Brigade. I work for Colonel___. You can't touch me!"

The Captain, off-duty and drunk, was over six feet tall and more than 200 pounds. He was yelling in the face of the MP and poking him in the chest. The MPs wound up beating him down on a public street with their police batons.

But you know what? He got away with it. The Colonel "tossed him around" a little, but the Captain got off without any formal punishment. He'd assaulted a Korean girl in front of the police. He'd assaulted an MP from his own unit. But in the end, the Colonel protected him.

In this case:

Skill #1: Decide (1) if *you're* ready to talk about it, and (2) if the other person is ready. If you're the Captain, are *you* ready to talk things over at this moment? If you're honest, your answer would be "no." The Captain is too angry—and drunk.

- Even if your answer were "yes," your second question—is *the girl* ready or willing to talk things over?—would get "no" for an answer. She's too busy right now!

- If you were willing to see her another time—while sober, and while you'd have her to yourself—you could try Skill #1. But could you believe anything she'd tell you?

Skill #2: Talk to the person you're angry at (and keep everyone else out of it). Talking to *her* is better than dragging your friends in on the problem. But in this case, your friends might be more sympathetic than she will. And they may be more willing to listen to you! If your answers to Skill #1 are "no," you can't use Skill #2.

Skill #3: Pay attention to their feelings (as well as your own). This is not the time to ask how she feels! If your answers to Skills #1 are "no," Skill #3 won't work.

Skill #4: Find something in common. You and her other customer have more in common than you and she have! Again, without two "yesses" for Skill #1, you can't use Skill #4.

Skill #5: Depersonalize the situation. *This* is a good idea. Use all the steps to this skill. Her "involvement" with the other man is *not* because of anything about *you.*

Skill #6: Get to the *real* issue(s). This skill is important here. You've got *two* issues. The first is that you're angry. The second is that she does *not* want to work things out with you. She's *not* your girlfriend!

Skill #7: Drop the grudge. This is a good idea, too. You have to let go of your *fantasy* that she was your girlfriend. This can hurt your pride. And maybe your feelings. First, use the healing steps in "Letting Go of Grudges in General." Then, get back control of your anger—and your life.

If you're the person telling the story, you feel frustrated by how much the Captain got away with. You're angry about the injustice. You can use the skills in the following ways:

Skill #1: Decide (1) if *you're* ready to talk about it, and (2) if the other person is ready.
You're ready to talk. But neither the Captain nor the Colonel is. So Skill #1 won't work here.

Skill #2: Talk to the person you're angry at (and keep everyone else out of it). This won't work without Skill #1.

Skill #3: Pay attention to their feelings (as well as your own). This won't either.

Skill #4: Find something in common. Nor will this.

Skill #5: Depersonalize the situation. *This* is a good idea. Use all the steps to this skill. The Captain's behavior, and the Colonel's letting him get away with it, have nothing to do with *you*. *They* were wrong. But it was not about you.

Skill #6: Get to the *real* issue(s). This skill is important here. You've got several real issues. First, both the Captain and the Colonel were wrong. Second, you have no authority over either of them. Third, you're angry about the injustices they commited. Fourth, you're angry about not being able to do anything.

Skill #7: Drop the grudge. This is a good idea, too. You have to use the healing steps in "Letting Go of Grudges in General." You're right about the situation. But you have no power and must let go of this burden.

Road rage

It was one of those road rage things. A guy in a black Camaro cut me off and damn near ran into me. He was driving so fast I couldn't keep up with him, even though I tried. And he was doing it on purpose, I could tell. As fast as he was going, I felt like he had singled me out to pass. He pulled up and slid in front of me. I probably wouldn't have tried to catch him if I didn't know he had picked me out of all the cars on the road.

But here's the best part. A few days later, there he was again on the same freeway. I recognized him right away. This was my big chance. How often do you get a chance like that? I gunned the car as fast as it would go, got right up there next to him just like he'd done to me, and pulled right in front of him.

He tailgated me at 95 miles an hour. I had a hard time getting away from him.

In this case:

Skill #1: Decide (1) if *you're* ready to talk about it, and (2) if the other person is ready. If you're the driver telling the story, the answers to both questions are "no." You're in a situation that's hardly safe for *driving,* much less *talking.* And it sounds like both of you are in the same mindset. Skill #1 won't work.

Skill #2: Talk to the person you're angry at (and keep everyone else out of it). You can't use this skill unless Skill #1 is working.

Skill #3: Pay attention to their feelings (as well as your own). Nor this one.

Skill #4: Find something in common. All you have in common with this driver is that you're both driving dangerously. *You're* taking his driving too personally. Only *he* knows what's really going on in his mind—in *spite* of the fact that you think his driving is aimed at *you.*

Skill #5: Depersonalize the situation. *This* skill is important for you. This person *may or may not* be the same driver. Maybe it's a different person and he thinks—correctly—that *you're* starting a problem with *him*. Even if it *is* the same person, you're assuming he's still after *you*.

You'll be much better off if you stop taking his driving *personally*. Whether it's the same man or not, he's just driving in his own self-centered way. And it's really self-centered of *you* to think he'd go to this much trouble (and risk) just for you.

Skill #6: Get to the *real* issue(s). The first real issue is that you're taking very personally some other man's driving. The second real issue is that you don't even know if it's the same person—so you may be "getting even" with an innocent driver. The third real issue is that no matter who the driver is, *you're* putting your own life—and possibly *others'* lives—at great risk. For no reason. And the fourth real issue is that—hard as it is on your ego to hear this—*you're really not important enough for any driver to be trying to "get."* It's not because of anything wrong with *you*. It's because *no one* is important enough for a stranger to be after him on the road.

Skill #7: Drop the grudge. All the steps in this skill will help you. The section "How to Drop the Grudge So You Can Act Now" will help you get past your ego and focus on being a better driver. The section on "How to Drop the Grudge When the Other Person Wants to Get You" will help. The section on "Letting Go of Grudges in General" will help you get rid of the huge chip on your shoulder that makes you think complete strangers are out to get you.

And the section on "Grieving" may help you get past your need to pretend you're "*so* important." You're *no less* important than anyone else. But there's no reason to think you're any *more* important, either.

Angry at a drunk

A radio call went out early in the morning: "Officer needs backup at _____." Everyone responds, and when I arrive there are already 3 or 4 units there. Officer X has a belligerent drunk handcuffed and the other units are dealing with the drunken passengers.

Officer X's drunk is seated on the edge of the rear seat, his legs and feet outside the car. He's refusing to put them inside. He just doesn't want to go to jail. He's not kicking, thrashing, or being aggressive. He's just refusing to put his legs in the car and go to jail.

Suddenly, Officer X pulls out his baton and starts beating on the man's legs and knees. The officer's face was bright red, and he was screaming and swearing as he swung his stick, THWACK, THWACK.

The drunk isn't doing anything but screaming in pain as the blows keep coming.

Officer X has totally lost it. I'm thinking he's going for the man's head next. I grab Officer X and pull him away. He loses his balance and tumbles backwards. Suddenly, he's coming after ME!

He's screaming and yelling, "Don't EVER touch me, you son-of-a-bitch! Don't EVER touch me!"

I try to explain why I pulled him off, but he's still pumped.

I retreat back to my car. Officer X eventually turned away and calmed down. Other officers got the drunk inside the car during this drama.

Nothing ever came of the incident. Officer X went up the promotional ladder. He eventually became a high-ranking officer in the department. On those few occasions when we've met, neither he nor I ever discussed the incident. I've wondered if he even remembers it—but I believe he does.

Ironically, the week before this incident, we had an officer fired and prosecuted for striking a drunk driver in the mouth with his baton. This was fresh in my mind at the time.

In this case:

Skill #1: Decide (1) if *you're* ready to talk about it, and (2) if the other person is ready. If you're the officer telling the story, it's clear that *you* want to talk, but Officer X *doesn't*. Skill #1 doesn't work in this scenario.

Skill #2: Talk to the person you're angry at (and keep everyone else out of it). You can't use this skill unless Skill #1 works.

Skill #3: Pay attention to their feelings (as well as your own). You can't help but *notice* his anger! But it won't work to try to *talk* about it. Officer X is too far *into* it.

Skill #4: Find something in common. It's real clear what you both have in common right now—dealing with the drunk. But *you've* also got *Officer X* to deal with!

Skill #5: Depersonalize the situation. *This* is important here. You have to realize—in your guts as well as your mind—that Officer X is doing his *own* thing. It has *nothing* to do with *you*.

Skill #6: Get to the *real* issue(s). Right now, you've got *three* real issues: the drunk, Officer X, and your need to take care of the drunk *in spite of* Officer X. Because of your role as an officer, and because of the situation, the *third* real issue is the one you've got to work on at the moment.

Skill #7: Drop the grudge. Take the steps under "How to Drop the Grudge So You Can Act Now." You have to carry out your role as a police officer. So get past Officer X. Get help, and do whatever you must to take care of the drunk.

Later, when you get home, use the steps under "How to Let Go of Grudges in General." They will help you let go of any anger you kept inside.

Personal attacks

This man in the bar was pissed, God knows why, and got in my face for no reason at all. I knew he was drunk, so I tried to ignore him. But then he started to say things, not about me, but about my wife! He said some pretty filthy and nasty things about her. He said how he knew where I lived and he'd been watching my wife for a while. He got into how turned on he got watching her and what he was going to do to her. The more disgusting he got, the angrier I got.

Now this man had no idea who I was or where I lived.

There was no way he could have ever seen my wife. I knew this as he mouthed off. Yet I started shaking, that's how angry I got. I could feel the muscles in my face twitching and my body tensing. My heart was beginning to beat harder and I had trouble talking.

I should have just walked away. This wasn't even really about me or my wife. And I knew it. But instead I hit him. And you know what's worse? I even started getting suspicious about my wife going out on me.

In this case:

Skill #1: Decide (1) if *you're* ready to talk about it, and (2) if the other person is ready. If you were the man listening to the drunk, you clearly were *not* ready to talk things over with the drunk. And the drunk was in no shape to talk things over with you. Skill #1 won't work here.

Skill #2: Talk to the person you're angry at (and keep everyone else out of it). You can't do this unless Skill #1 is working.

Skill #3: Pay attention to their feelings (as well as your own). You're already paying *too much* attention to the drunk's feelings! And you're taking them too personally.

Skill #4: Find something in common. All you have in common right now is that neither of you is being rational. This skill won't work without Skill #1.

Skill #5: Depersonalize the situation. *This* skill is *extremely* important for you—and for your marriage!

Skill #6: Get to the *real* issue(s). The first real issue is that you took a drunk's words seriously and personally, even though you *knew* he didn't know what he was talking about! The drunk's words had more to do with *him* and *his* life than with you and yours. Stop "owning" problems that aren't yours.

The second real issue is that you put *yourself* at risk—physically and legally—when you hit him. For nothing.

Skill #7: Drop the grudge. You have *nothing* to hold a grudge about. Use the steps under "How to Let Go of a Grudge and Act Now." Also use the steps under "How to Drop the Grudge When the Other Person Wants to Get You." The action you should use right now is to get up and leave *before* you let the drunk get to you. Later, use the steps under "How to Let Go of Grudges in General." The drunk's words triggered something in you that you need to let go of.

Challenges to your authority—while you're under stress

I had just learned of the death of a friend—a fellow officer—in a helicopter crash. He and another officer had been working an area in the mountains nearby, and as the sun was setting, my friend didn't see the power lines and flew into them.

Both men were cremated in the crash.

When I found out, I was stunned. I remember asking myself how I should respond. I remember feeling as if I couldn't breathe. But I had no desire to weep, shout, hit the wall, or anything else. I remember one officer asking me what was wrong, because he must have seen something in my face.

In any case, I didn't have time to dwell on it, because the Sheriff's Department was requesting backup and traffic-control in a remote area where they were in the process of closing down a huge "party." More than 1,500 kids were drunk.

I responded to the area call and was amazed at the number of cars trying to get to this party—there were hundreds of them. My task was to take up a position at an intersection and route the cars LEFT, away from the party on the RIGHT.

The Sheriff's Department was sweeping them out of the area and obviously didn't want more cars coming in.

To say the least, it was—in police jargon—a "cluster-fuck."

I had been in position for about five minutes. Drivers were reluctantly following my traffic-control directions and turning away from the area as directed. All had nasty comments as they passed by, but things were going as well as could be expected.

I was very tired. I was wishing all this would end. I just wanted to go home.

And then, one car stopped and nudged towards the right. I stopped it and saw that it was two young kids, female.

I approached the right side and told them, "The party's over. Turn left and leave the area."

One girl looked at the other, said something, and began to slowly continue turning to the right. I repeated my directions and again they said something to each other, but didn't move.

Then I saw that all the other cars were watching. I knew full well that if I let one car through, it would be an unstoppable torrent of teenagers. I turned up the volume and told the girls, "If you don't turn left and leave, this [my baton] is going through your window! Now get the hell out of here, NOW!"

The next thing I knew, they had gunned the engine, were turning right—and I did what I said I'd do. I slammed my baton through their rear window as they passed (nearly running over my foot). Well, glass flew all over the place. They stopped and began screaming hysterically.

About that time, another car slid into where we were, and out jumps the boyfriend. He was the last thing I needed at the scene. I yelled something to him about having one second to leave or he was going to jail for interfering. He made some verbal threats, but did in fact get back in his car and leave.

I called for a supervisor. I managed to get the now-crying and sobbing girls calmed down. I took their identification as I knew there would be lots of paperwork. Fortunately, the Sheriff's deputies had cleared out the area and the scene was stable. I returned to the office, wrote up a memo on the incident, and went home.

I don't know if you've ever tried to break a car window with a straight piece of hickory. It is damned near impossible.

It usually just bounces off. I recall my baton just passing through the glass with nearly no resistance whatsoever. I was obviously pumped up and full of adrenaline.

There wasn't, and probably never will be, any specific training that would prepare an officer for dealing with this kind of overt defiance while directing traffic. But the failure was mine. I had just heard about my friend's death in the helicopter, and I "sucked it up" and went back to work.

Later, when I asked the Captain what I should have done instead about the kids, he said he didn't know either.

In this case:

Skill #1: Decide (1) if *you're* ready to talk about it, and (2) if the other person is ready. If you're the officer, it will be clear that no one is ready to talk about it—not you, not the girls, not the boyfriend, not the rest of the traffic.

Skill #2: Talk to the person you're angry at (and keep everyone else out of it). This skill can't happen, because Skill #1 isn't working.

Skill #3: Pay attention to their feelings (as well as your own). You're having to pay much *more* attention to the girls' (and boyfriend's, and other drivers') feelings than you want to! But there's no room here for you to *talk* about it with any of them.

Skill #4: Find something in common. This won't work here either. At the moment, there are far more *differences* than things in common between you and them. Even if you tried to talk about safety, no one's listening.

Skill #5: Depersonalize the situation. This skill is *crucial* to you in this situation. You have to *know* in your guts that the situation is way out of control. Even with your stress and exhaustion, the problems are *not* caused by *you*.

Skill #6: Get to the *real* issue(s). There are a *number* of real issues:

1. You're still in shock from your friend's sudden and tragic death. You are *not* able to think clearly or deal with the stress, *right now*.

2. The traffic is far greater than you *or anyone* can handle alone.

3. The girls and the boyfriend "just wanna have fun," are too self-centered to care about the law, and are too young to worry about safety.

Skill #7: Drop the grudge. You have *three* grudges here—rightfully.

1. Because of the shock about your friend's death, you shouldn't even have been on the job. But real life doesn't wait for us. All you could do *right then* is use the steps under "Drop the Grudge So You Can Act Right Now." They will help make it easier for you to do what you have to do right then. Later, the steps under "How to Drop the Grudge When the Other Person Wants to Get

You" will help you see things more clearly. So will "Letting Go of Grudges in General."

Later, when you get home, use the steps under "Grieving." They'll help you start healing from the loss of your friend.

2. The amount of traffic is *beyond your control.* The same steps will help you do what you have to do now.

3. The girls' short-term thinking is *beyond your control.* Again, the steps under "Drop the Grudge So You Can Act Right Now" will help.

4. Give yourself some *credit* for how you dealt with the boyfriend and the girls. *It worked.* Even the Captain said he didn't know what else could have been done.

The key issue here is not so much what the police officer did, but that he did it in anger and *lost control.* Sometimes, you're faced with a no-win situation. You have no control over that—but you *do* have the ability to control *yourself.*

Pent-up anger

The boss had favored this employee for years. There were rumors that the employee "had" something on the boss, but we never knew for sure. What we did know was that the employee was a lousy worker and the boss covered up for him.

There wasn't much we could do about it, so most of us just blew it off. But another co-worker resented the whole situation and his resentment grew every time the problem employee got away with something.

One day, the resentful co-worker lost it and threatened the problem employee.

"You get paid as much as the rest of us, but we're all doing your work for you," he said. "I've had it. You're gonna find your-self dead in the parking lot one of these days."

He's the one who got fired, not the problem worker.

In this case:

Skill #1: Decide (1) if *you're* ready to talk about it, and (2) if the other person is ready. If you were the resentful co-worker who blew up, you'd have to say "no" to both questions. You can't talk to the person about your anger because you have no authority over him. And he doesn't care about your problem. Skill #1 won't work here.

Skill #2: Talk to the person you're angry at (and keep everyone else out of it). You can't do this unless Skill #1 is working.

Skill #3: Pay attention to their feelings (as well as your own). Because Skills #1 and, therefore, #2 aren't working, you can't do this either.

Skill #4: Find something in common. Nor this one.

Skill #5: Depersonalize the situation. *This* is a skill you *can* use. And *must.* It's natural to resent the person. But the situation is out of your control. He's not even doing anything "to" *you.* You resent how the boss favors him. But—as much as this may hurt your pride—it's not about *you.* Even though your boss is unfair, and even though the person doesn't deserve special treatment, neither of them care how it affects *you.*

All you can do is admit, to yourself, that you *don't like* the situation. Or that you don't want to work under these conditions. You can complain to Human Resources, or your boss's boss, about being ignored. But you *can't change* the way your boss treats your co-worker.

Skill #6: Get to the *real* issue(s). The real issues are:

1. Your boss unfairly favors a co-worker for reasons unknown to you.

2. You resent the situation—and the co-worker.

3. You take the situation too personally, as if it were *aimed at you.*

4. You lost control of your anger and let *it* take charge of *you.*

5. Your threat made *you* the problem. *You* threatened a co-worker. Your action was much more *direct,* as well as physically threatening, than anything the co-worker did to you.

6. You lost your job because *you* became the problem.

7. Because of (6), you let the person "win" even *more.*

Skill #7: Drop the grudge. If you had this all to do over again, you could use the steps under "How to Drop the Grudge So You Can Act Now." They'd help you detach more from what you can't control. They'd help you blow it off like your other co-workers did.

Now you need the steps under "Letting Go of Grudges in General"— and under "Grieving."

Cover-ups

Some soldiers were arrested downtown by the civilian police for allegedly assaulting a Korean civilian. They were processed and turned over to us, but they were on "hold" because the Korean authorities maintained jurisdiction over the offense. We could take no formal action to punish or investigate the assault.

Two weeks later, more facts came out. One of the soldiers, the night before he was arrested, was approached in the same downtown area by on-duty military police. The soldier was drunk. He was assaulting a Korean civilian—an old man selling flowers. To top it off, he was belligerent to the MPs, drunk, and disorderly. No report was ever made of this.

The next night, when he was arrested for assaulting the other person, everyone kept their mouths shut. A U.S. Army staff sergeant, on-duty, in uniform, and charged with the responsibility to maintain law and order, allowed a drunk soldier to assault a Korean—the sergeant took no action other than sending the soldier on his way.

In this case:

Skill #1: Decide (1) if *you're* ready to talk about it, and (2) if the other person is ready. If you're the soldier who describes this case, the politics may stop you from telling the sergeant how angry you are about the injustices he allowed. But even if you *want* to, the odds are high that he *won't* want to talk with *you* about it. Skill #1 probably won't work here.

Skill #2: Talk to the person you're angry at (and keep everyone else out of it). This skill won't take place unless *both* of you are willing to talk.

Skill #3: Pay attention to their feelings (as well as your own). This skill won't work without Skill #1.

Skill #4: Find something in common. Again, no action without Skill #1.

Skill #5: Depersonalize the situation. *This* is the first step you *can* take. As right as you are, this injustice is *not your issue.* At least, not in terms of you talking to the sergeant. It's not because of *you.* It's your *position* and *role.* The sergeant doesn't have to answer to a soldier. *Period.*

Another choice you have is to go higher up on the chain-of-command. You even could write to your congressman. But remember the politics before you decide whether to do this. Sometimes it's worth the risk—and sometimes it's not.

Skill #6: Get to the *real* issue(s). You have *two* real issues right now. The first is that you're angry because the sergeant allowed two injustices. The second is that you have no authority and can't do much about it.

Skill #7: Drop the grudge. For both real issues, use the steps under "Let Go of Grudges in General." The "grudge" you're dropping is about not being able to control things.

Scapegoat

One of the men in the crew was the type that got along with everyone. You know, the kind of guy that's easygoing and doesn't let anything bother him, joking a lot and taking the pressure off everyone.

He had a favorite jacket, and we always kidded him about it because he wore it whether it was hot or cold out. One day, for no reason at all, another man on the crew—who nobody liked—took this guy's jacket and threw it into the concrete pour.

When he saw what happened to his jacket, he got real quiet and never really was the same for the rest of the time he worked with us. We missed the good times we'd had.

And for what?

In this case:

Skill #1: Decide (1) if *you're* ready to talk about it, and (2) if the other person is ready. If you were the man who lost the jacket, you didn't even have a chance to ask yourself these questions. The bully took his anger out on you without any warning. So Skill #1 won't work here.

Skill #2: Talk to the person you're angry at (and keep everyone else out of it). This only works when you can use Skill #1.

Skill #3: Pay attention to their feelings (as well as your own). You didn't have a chance to do this. He acted out his feelings before you knew what they were.

Skill #4: Find something in common. This won't work either.

Skill #5: Depersonalize the situation. *This* skill is important to protect your own feelings. The man used *you* as a scapegoat for his anger. It *wasn't* about *you.*

Skill #6: Get to the *real* issue(s). The real issue is that you have no control over people who take their problems out on innocent bystanders.

Skill #7: Drop the grudge. You have three sources of anger now. One, you lost the jacket, which was important to you—the good times. Two, you lost the good atmosphere at work. Three, even if you do something to "get even," it doesn't solve the other two problems, and it could make things worse for you.

For right now, you can use the steps under "How to Drop the Grudge So You Can Act Now." They will help you today.

Later, you can use the steps under both "Letting Go of Grudges in General" and "Grieving." If you *don't* take these steps, you risk feeling angry, hurt, and less upbeat than you deserve. These steps will help you regain the good feelings and good friendships you had before the jacket incident.

Harassment

This soldier was in the barracks getting drunk. He took a permanent marker and wrote the words "You nasty ho" on the door of a female soldier across the hall. She was in the same battalion, but in a different company.

This incident wasn't reported. Nobody said a thing. But the story came out a week later. I sat down with the battalion commander—a Lieutenant Colonel—and the Command Sergeant Major, and told them about this. I was ordered to take no action. The CSM said, "Maybe she really is a nasty ho."

On top of that, the battalion commander didn't want any heat because he already was getting negative attention from his boss because of other similar problems in the battalion. He didn't want to risk more exposure.

So an incident of sexual harassment and vandalism was allowed to go unpunished because it might make him look bad.

And here's what happened some months later. The same soldier was out drinking to celebrate his last night in the unit. He was in the club on the base and he punched a girl and knocked her unconscious.

The MPs responded and took him in. The new company commander dropped all charges.

"When he gets on that plane," he said, "he's not our problem anymore."

In this case:

Skill #1: Decide (1) if *you're* ready to talk about it, and (2) if the other person is ready. If you're the soldier describing the situation, you're angry at the misbehaving soldier, the first Commander, the Lieutenant Colonel, the CMS, and the new Commander. The politics may be against talking to any of them. But even if you want to, the odds are very slim that any of them will talk to you. Skill #1 doesn't work here.

Skill #2: Talk to the person you're angry at (and keep everyone else out of it). This won't work without Skill #1.

Skill #3: Pay attention to their feelings (as well as your own). Again, you can't do this without Skill #1.

Skill #4: Find something in common. Nor this.

Skill #5: Depersonalize the situation. *This* skill will help you. You have to accept the fact that you are right to be angry. But you *also* have to remember that it's not about you. It wasn't aimed at you. Only the targets of the harassment—in this case, the woman soldier and the second woman—might have a chance of filing a complaint. *You* can't do anything about this event.

Skill #6: Get to the *real* issue(s). The real issues are:

1. The soldier committed harassment, vandalism, and assault.

2. The officers in charge—several levels up—let him get away with these acts.

3. You're angry because they let him get away with what he did.

4. You can't do anything about it.

Skill #7: Drop the grudge. The steps under "Letting Go of Grudges in General" will help you a lot. You have to take these steps, to be able to let go of what you can't control.

Being set up

My boss makes himself look good by blaming everyone else for his mistakes. I was on a team in charge of setting up a new computer system. We did the technical installation, after all the decisions were made and the equipment had been picked.

When things didn't work as well or as smoothly as they were supposed to, my boss blamed my team. But the truth was that he had failed to do all the research he was supposed to do—who needed what kind of services, which types of equipment worked best together, you know, all the important stuff you have to know before you can make good decisions about computers.

If he'd gotten all the information, the decision-makers would have chosen different equipment. But the technical team got blamed for problems that really came from buying the wrong stuff.

The worst part is, you have to be pretty technical yourself before you can understand what the real problem is. To most people in the company, the team looks like we don't know how to do our jobs.

So you know what I did? I made sure my boss's computer had the worst problems. If he's going to complain about us anyway, I'll give him good reason to complain!

In this case:

Skill #1: Decide (1) if *you're* ready to talk about it, and (2) if the other person is ready. If you're the employee telling the story, the answers to both questions are "no." You might have tried to talk things over with your boss the first or second time he blamed the employees for everything. But even if you tried in the past, you know now that he doesn't want to change what he's doing, so he's not going to talk it over with you.

Skill #2: Talk to the person you're angry at (and keep everyone else out of it). You need Skill #1 for this to work.

Skill #3: Pay attention to their feelings (as well as your own). This won't work either.

Skill #4: Find something in common. Neither will this.

Skill #5: Depersonalize the situation. *This* skill will help. You already know that the problem is *not* you or the rest of the technical team. The problem involves egos, politics, and bureaucracy—*not* you.

Skill #6: Get to the *real* issue(s). The real issues are:

1. Your boss blames you and the rest of the technical team for problems that really came from him and the decision-making process.

2. Other people in the organization don't have enough information to understand that you and the team are *not* to blame.

3. Up to this point, the problem is *not* about *you.* However, as soon as you started to mess with your boss's computer, you *lost control* of your anger and let *it* take charge of *you.*

4. By letting your anger control you, *you* became the *second* problem. Although you have to depersonalize the actions of your boss and the decision-makers, you *are* responsible for what *you* did.

Skill #7: Drop the grudge. You could use the steps under "How to Drop the Grudge So You Can Act Now." They'll help you create a S-P-A-C-E between *feeling* your anger and taking any *action.* So will the steps under "How to Drop the Grudge When the Other Person Wants to Get You." Later, the steps under "Letting Go of Grudges in General" can help you get past the general problems of egos and politics in organizations.

But by messing with your boss's computer, you're creating more problems for yourself, because your secret way of getting even *also keeps you stuck in anger.* Go back to Skill #7, learn to let go, and fix the problem you created—for your boss *and* for yourself.

Needing to show off

I was in charge of a detail to provide traffic control for an annual event. The road also led to a big park. The temperature was hot and humid.

Traffic backs up. People drink at the park and at the fair. The country roads are clogged with hot, angry drivers. At least four major accidents occurred here per day, making law enforcement nearly impossible. Most days, we ran around scraping people off the road and then writing the report.

Near sunset, at the intersection, I was directing traffic. This was a four-way stop and sorely in need of a traffic light. People do not like to wait in line—especially after a long hot day in the sun and a few beers. They do crazy stuff.

Directing traffic is a special kind of hell for a police officer. It's not real police work. You're a target—both emotionally and physically—in the middle of an intersection. You need to have lots of psychic energy and attention. It's physically draining.

All my crew had left the detail. We'd thought the bulk of the traffic was gone. But I made one last check of the intersection. It was backed up about two miles—to a notoriously dangerous area. Someone will get hurt up there, I thought.

I also thought of my wife and kids at home, my tired body, and my frayed nerves. But I stayed and finished my job anyway.

Something wasn't right. Traffic so heavy this late. I kept directing traffic and it still wouldn't go away. Then I saw three motorcycles driving on the wrong side of the road, passing all traffic. They were approaching my position.

Ah! Finally, a chance to do real police work, I thought. I'd hammer these guys, get all three. If I'm lucky, they'll run and I can go in pursuit. Wouldn't that be fun!

I directed them to the right shoulder. Next, to the police car where I felt safe, and my "pinch" book. I was charged. I remember the extreme excitement. Heart pounding, shaking at the edge of control. Of course, I didn't pay attention to what it meant. I was trained not to trust emotions. One must be in control at all times. I had been a police officer for about five years, and was confident.

I also was confident about my ability to control suspects—even three of them. They all pulled over. The leader rode up next to me and remained astride his bike. The other two held back and dismounted about 20 feet away.

Enforcement tactics now were in the shitter. With three violators who were split, I was in a bad position. They could have just robbed a store, for all I knew, and could be pulling weapons out of their leather jackets.

The leader grinned as he said, "What's the problem, Officer?"

I remember raising my voice—something I had never done with the public before. I remember his grin falling from his face.

I asked him for his license and registration. He regained his composure, smiled again, and slapped me on the stomach with the back of his hand.

"Take it easy," he said to me. "This is just a big game, you know."

Things get real fuzzy for me here. I remember impressions.

The violator said, "You wouldn't be so tough without that badge." I took my badge off and threw it into the police car.

The violator said, "You wouldn't be so tough without the gun." I took off my gun-belt, with weapons, and threw it into the police car.

The violator—not grinning anymore—said, "What are you going to do, beat me up?"

I said, "This is not a game. Get off your bike and give me your license."

The violator—with a look of shock on his face—said, "I think you would beat me up. And probably enjoy it, too."

I said, "You bet your fucking ass I would. Now give me me your license and shut the fuck up." My voice was just below rage. It felt so good to finally stand up and show someone how I really felt.

The other two quickly jumped on their bikes and left. I wrote the man a citation. I felt naked and powerful, not needing those symbols of power.

But the ticket was just another act of stupidity, because now the man had written proof of our encounter. He could easily cause the end of my promising career.

On the way home, I felt fear and guilt. Just two more emotions to stuff.

In this case:

Skill #1: Decide (1) if *you're* ready to talk about it, and (2) if the other person is ready. If you're the officer, you'd have to admit that the biker is more willing—and able — to work things out than you are. You're too exhausted and stressed out. *And* too angry. Even if the biker's answer to question (2) is "yes," *your* answer to question (1) is "no." So Skill #1 won't work here.

Skill #2: Talk to the person you're angry at (and keep everyone else out of it). You *are* talking to him. But you're too angry to be on top of the situation—*or* yourself. This skill can't work without Skill #1.

Skill #3: Pay attention to their feelings (as well as your own). The biker seems to know more about how you feel than *you* do right now. And *he* even tried to calm *you* down. You can't use this skill when Skill #1 doesn't work.

Skill #4: Find something in common. You need Skill #1 for this one also.

Skill #5: Depersonalize the situation. *This* is a skill you can use right now. Your exhaustion hurt your self-control. You *made* the scene more personal than you needed to. And you're *taking* it too personally, also.

Skill #6: Get to the *real* issue(s). The first real issue is that you're tired. The second real issue is that the other officers left too soon—you needed backup. The third issue is that you let things get too personal—*you* were out to get *them*.

Skill #7: Drop the grudge. When you were face-to-face with the biker, the steps under "How to Drop the Grudge So You Can Act Now" would help. So would the steps under "How to Drop the Grudge When the Other Person Wants to Get You." When you get home, use "Letting Go of Grudges in General" to help you take things less personally.

Looking good

There were new soldiers in the battalion who had not yet qualified on their weapons. This is a readiness problem that needs to get fixed. The company commander arranged for these soldiers to go to a marksmanship range with the brigade headquarters company. This is common practice—we often share ranges to help everyone out.

The battalion commander found out, however, and would not allow it. His justification, at a staff meeting that included his key subordinate leaders, was: "If our soldiers go to that range and do something 'wrong', the brigade commander might see them. That will make us look bad."

He was really talking about himself, of course. What is the lesson the subordinate leaders are supposed to learn from this? He would rather let the unit's wartime readiness suffer than risk "looking bad."

In this case:

Skill #1: Decide (1) if _you're_ ready to talk about it, and (2) if the other person is ready. If you're the person telling the story, you don't have much chance to talk things over with the battalion commander. Because of the difference in rank, the answer to both questions is "no."

Skill #2: Talk to the person you're angry at (and keep everyone else out of it). Because Skill #1 won't work, you can't do this.

Skill #3: Pay attention to their feelings (as well as your own). Nor this.

Skill #4: Find something in common. This won't work either.

Skill #5: Depersonalize the situation. _This_ step helps you keep your sanity when the situation is stupid but out of your control. You're right, the battalion commander is wrong—but it's _not_ about _you._ So you can't do anything.

Skill #6: Get to the *real* issue(s). The first real issue is that you're angry at the battalion commander. The second real issue is that you're angry at being unable to *do* anything about it.

Skill #7: Drop the grudge. To help you get through the moment, you can use the steps under "How to Drop the Grudge So You Can Act Now." Later, for your general frustration, use the steps under "Letting Go of Grudges in General." They'll help you accept the things you can't control.

Unclear goals

I've had this job for five years, and every performance review is the same. I "need to be more professional" or "need improvement" in some area, but it's never clear exactly what that means I'm supposed to do.

When I ask my boss, all he says is more of the same general things. "You know, do a better job with our customers" or "Handle that problem more professionally." When I ask him what "a better job" or "more professionally" would look like, he gets angry and tells me to "stop avoiding the issues."

He's got no right to get angry. But I do! So I just stick to my job duties and don't do a single extra thing.

In this case:

Skill #1: Decide (1) if *you're* ready to talk about it, and (2) if the other person is ready. If you're the employee, your answer to both questions is "no." You've kept trying to find out more, but your boss seems unable to make things more clear.

Skill #2: Talk to the person you're angry at (and keep everyone else out of it). This won't work without Skill #1. You've already tried, anyway.

Skill #3: Pay attention to their feelings (as well as your own). You need Skill #1 for this, also.

Skill #4: Find something in common. This won't work either, without Skill #1.

Skill #5: Depersonalize the situation. *This* skill will help. You're the one living with the problem, but you're *not* the cause. At the same time, *you'll* have to figure out a way to solve it, because your boss can't.

Skill #6: Get to the *real* issue(s). The real issues are:

1. Your boss is too vague about what he wants you to improve.

2. You're angry about it, but can't fix it.

3. You "get even" by withdrawing from the job and doing only as much as you "have to."

4. By doing (3), you're hurting yourself. People can't pick and choose what feelings to have. We feel either *all* our feelings, or *none*. So if you shut yourself off at work to "get even," you're also hurting *yourself.* You can't feel *good* while you're feeling *shut off.*

5. You'll have to get help from Human Resources or another source at work. You'll be able to do this *only* if you feel good enough to do it *and* get past your anger.

Skill #7: Drop the grudge. For the moment, use the steps under "How to Drop a Grudge and Act *Now*" to get past your anger and do the best you can on your job. Later, use the steps under "Letting Go of Grudges in General" to get rid of the chip on your shoulder and come back to life. Then, go to Human Resources, or another source, at work and get help for you and your boss.

Treated "special"

One day, after 9/11, the Colonel's wife was waiting in line at the gate. All security was tightened and the gates were under heavy guard.

The wife was displeased about the wait and the fact that she was being treated like everyone else. She gave the MP at the gate a piece of her mind. Afterwards, she called her husband.

The Colonel immediately called the MP's supervisor and relieved him of his duties—right there in front of his soldiers. There was no investigation or questioning. The only cause was the irate phone call from his wife.

In this case:

Skill #1: Decide (1) if *you're* ready to talk about it, and (2) if the other person is ready. If you're another soldier describing the situation, your answer to both questions is "no." Because the Colonel has authority over you, you can't tell him how angry you are about what he did.

Skill #2: Talk to the person you're angry at (and keep everyone else out of it). You can't do this without Skill #1.

Skill #3: Pay attention to their feelings (as well as your own). You can't do this without Skill #1, either.

Skill #4: Find something in common. Nor this.

Skill #5: Depersonalize the situation. *This* skill will help you. The Colonel was wrong to let his wife skip the security steps. And he was wrong to stop the MP from doing his job—and for yelling at the MP in front of his soldiers. But this has nothing to do with *you* personally. Even if you were the MP. It's about the Colonel, and it's about his wife. It's *not* about *you*.

Skill #6: Get to the *real* issue(s). The real issues are:

1. The wife had no business wanting special treatment.

2. The Colonel was wrong to give his wife special treatment.

3. The Colonel should not have stopped the MP.

4. The Colonel should not have yelled at the MP for doing the right thing—especially in front of his soldiers.

5. You're angry about (1) through (4).

Skill #7: Drop the grudge. Right now, use the steps under "How to Drop the Grudge So You Can Act Now." They will help you carry out your job. Later, use the steps under "Letting Go of Grudges in General." They will help you deal with the things you can't control.

Being silenced

My company drug-tested all applicants and also current employees whose behavior was questionable. My department kept drug-test results on file.

In doing my job, I ran across a report that was inaccurate. It stated that the individual—an applicant—had tested negative for all the drugs, but I remembered that she actually had tested positive for cocaine.

When I told my boss about the error, she looked away and said, "No, that's not true. You remember it incorrectly."

I started to tell her about the original report, which I'd seen a few days after the applicant filled out the forms, but my boss looked at me and said, very firmly, "That is not correct. You must be thinking of a different report or another applicant."

I wasn't surprised to find out later that the applicant was the daughter of one of the executives. But I was angry that the executives could get away with making an exception that put everyone at risk—and that my boss was in on the cover-up.

So I told everyone who would listen, including the people who write the company newsletter. And—can you believe this?—suddenly I'm told that my job is now on third shift. They've done all the paperwork to justify the move, but you know the real reason is to shut me up.

In this case:

Skill #1: Decide (1) if *you're* ready to talk about it, and (2) if the other person is ready. If you're the employee, you already tried to tell the truth. Your boss won't let you. So your answers to both questions are "no."

Skill #2: Talk to the person you're angry at (and keep everyone else out of it). You already tried. This won't work without Skill #1.

Skill #3: Pay attention to their feelings (as well as your own). This won't work without Skill #1 either.

Skill #4: Find something in common. Neither will this.

Skill #5: Depersonalize the situation. *This* skill is important. Your boss, and the organizational politics and egos, are to blame. You did the right thing in trying to keep the records accurate. *Up to this point,* it's *not* about *you.*

But, as soon as you started to tell "everyone," you let your *anger* take charge of *you.* You lost control of your anger, and that's what led to your being silenced.

Skill #6: Get to the *real* issue(s). The real issues are:

1. You were right about the inaccuracy of the records.

2. You were right to point this out and try to correct it.

3. When you started telling "everyone," you let your anger take charge of your judgment. If you'd thought about it more calmly, you might have continued to push the issue, but in a quieter way—and only to people who might have been able to change things. You spoke out— to "everyone"—before you made a S-P-A-C-E to think about the best way to try to make things right.

4. You're stuck in a situation where management *doesn't* want the truth out. Politics and egos are more important to them.

Skill #7: Drop the grudge. The worst thing about the whole situation is that you got in trouble for doing the *right* thing. Your anger is justified. But holding on to your anger is bad for *you.* You want to let go of the anger for your sake. The steps under "Letting Go of Grudges in General" will help. So will the steps under "How to Drop the Grudge When the Other Person Wants to Get You."

And, unfair as this is, you may want to look somewhere else for a job. You've found out the nasty truth about your company's top management, not just your boss. It could be bad for you to have to face this every day—especially on a shift you don't want. The section entitled "Grieving" will help you accept this change.

Lack of professionalism

During my first month of company command, the Army changed headgear from the old "patrol cap" to the new black berets as part of a symbolic transformation.

On a Friday afternoon, my operations sergeant held a class for the younger soldiers. The purpose of the class was to teach them how to wear the new hat properly—it's not as simple as just putting it on your head. I was at a staff meeting, but I trusted the staff sergeant to do a good job.

A week or two later, everyone wore the new berets for the first time at a rehearsal for our "transformation ceremony."

None of the young soldiers had prepared their berets, and none of them wore the berets properly.

I took the staff sergeant aside and asked him why the soldiers had problems with the berets, following the class.

"It's common now, Sir," the staff sergeant replied. "You know soldiers never pay attention when they're getting a class."

I absolutely lost it. I was shocked that a professional soldier could say these words out loud. I went off on him bigger than shit. It seemed hypocritical to me for a so-called leader to even think this way.

In this case:

Skill #1: Decide (1) if *you're* ready to talk about it, and (2) if the other person is ready. If you're the Company Commander, your answer to the first question can—and should—be "yes." The staff sergeant reports to you, and it's part of your role to let him know when you have a problem with something he did or said. You also can assume that the staff sergeant's answer to the second question will be "yes." He reports to you, and if you want to talk about something, the odds are good that he'll comply.

Skill #2: Talk to the person you're angry at (and keep everyone else out of it). Tell him what you told us—that you find it unacceptable for a leader to think and say what he did. Remember that you're angry at what he *did*—*not* at him "in general."

Skill #3: Pay attention to their feelings (as well as your own). Let him know that you can understand his own anger, frustration, and other feelings if it was that hard to get the soldiers to learn new things.

Skill #4: Find something in common. You both want the soldiers to learn. You both want to be good leaders. You both want to figure out the real reasons the soldiers *aren't* learning. And you both want to fix it so they *will* learn. You and the staff sergeant have a *lot* in common.

Skill #5: Depersonalize the situation. What the staff sergeant said *wasn't* about *you*. He was venting his anger, frustration, and other negative feelings about what sounds like a frequent problem.

Skill #6: Get to the *real* issue(s). The real issues are:

1. The staff sergeant is venting his frustration and probably doesn't realize how disloyal or *un*-leader-like he sounds.

2. The *real* "real" issue is that the soldiers apparently are not learning as much, or as quickly, as they should.

3. You and the staff sergeant have to figure out why (2) is happening, and how to fix it.

4. *You* became *un*professional and *un*-leader-like when you lost control of your anger. You let your anger take charge of you.

Skill #7: Drop the grudge. Right now, use the steps under "How to Drop a Grudge So You Can Act Now." They'll help you detach from your own anger. Then you can work with the staff sergeant to solve the real problem of how to help soldiers learn.

Going inward

I'd been a surgeon for more than 30 years. I'd taught medical students how to perform surgeries. I'd written papers and spoken regularly at professional conferences. I was seen as an expert in my field.

But I started to notice some changes. They were small changes—very small. And they only happened once in a while, not all the time. But they were still important changes, and problems for me. I'd feel down, almost depressed, for no reason at all. It didn't happen very often. But it stayed with me longer than I was used to. Nothing sharp or strong. Just a generally low kind of feeling.

Then I started to feel changes in my hands. It was nothing anyone else could see, and I still did excellent work in the operating room. You couldn't tell from watching me work. But it was a new feeling inside my hands. I can only describe it as kind of a looseness, a tiny but nagging feeling of not having total control. My hands were still steady—but they didn't feel that way to me.

I felt scared. Depressed. Shocked. On the verge of being out of control.

I didn't know what was happening to me. Not knowing made everything worse. And I didn't miss the irony, either—the well-known doctor couldn't diagnose himself.

I felt caught in a whirlwind. Losing control made me more depressed. The depression made me feel more out of control. I kept going over and over it in my mind, asking myself what might it be, when did I first noticed it, what might it mean. I was afraid to tell my patients. I was afraid they'd lose faith in me. I didn't even know what to tell them. I didn't know what was happening.

When I finally saw my own doctor, it was diagnosed as early stages of Parkinson's disease. My wife, my family, felt shocked, scared, out of control. Just like I'd been feeling. But for me, the diagnosis was a relief. I finally knew what was going on.

But here was the shock for me. It wasn't until then that I realized how angry I'd been. As aware as I'd been of my fear, shock, and depression, I hadn't realized how much rage I'd also felt. About being out of control. About having symptoms I couldn't diagnose. About not knowing what was going on. I'd kept the anger inside, hidden even from myself. And the stress from all this bottled-up anger might have increased the degree, or progression, of the disease.

In this case:

Skill #1: Decide (1) if *you're* ready to talk about it, and (2) if the other person is ready. If you're the surgeon, the "conversation"—like the anger—will start *inside* you, not (yet) with anyone else. Skill #1 will work, because you're ready to acknowledge your anger.

Skill #2: Talk to the person you're angry at (and keep everyone else out of it). This skill doesn't apply here.

Skill #3: Pay attention to their feelings (as well as your own). *Your* feelings are all that matter right now. You realize that it's time to pay attention to them and deal with them.

Skill #4: Find something in common. This skill doesn't apply here, since no one else is involved with your anger. But you *do* realize that keeping your anger inside might worsen the disease. So you are motivated, which is the purpose of Skill #4.

Skill #5: Depersonalize the situation. Neither does this one.

Skill #6: Get to the *real* issue(s). You have several real issues:

1. Your anger is real and justified.

2. Keeping your anger inside is *your* natural way to handle your anger.

3. You're wise to realize that being angry—*and* keeping it inside— can increase your stress and worsen the Parkinson's disease.

4. You need to let yourself go inside when you're angry—*for a while.* Then, you need to find someone you trust who will *listen—without giving advice*—while you talk to them about it. Bringing your anger *out*—when *you're* ready—will help you get the support you need. It also may energize you.

5. You need to let yourself grieve. This includes accepting what you may lose. But it also includes getting on with your life—that is, *focusing on what you still have.* There's more about this under Skill #7, which is next.

Skill #7: Drop the grudge.

1. Letting go of control is similar to letting go of addictions or grudges. Your medical practice, your success as a doctor, and your surgical skills have depended on your ability to control your hands, your mind, and potentially risky situations. Losing that control means giving up a lot that is important to you.

2. The section on "Letting Go of Grudges in General" will help you. So will the section on "Grieving."

3. Remember to focus on what you still *have*—and on how you can still use it to continue in your work and your teaching. You also may want to find ways to donate your knowledge and skills to the community. *Giving* can lower your anger and increase your focus on what you *have*.

Father and son

My son was 16 then. I knew damn well he was going out with his buddies to drink and do drugs. So I locked him in his room that night. I told him that if he even thought about sneaking out, I'd beat the shit out of him.

Well, next thing I know, he's gone. Went out through the bedroom window. I was pissed. SO pissed that I thought about hunting him down. But you know what? I didn't even know where to go look for him.

So I waited up all night. I got angrier by the minute. He didn't get back 'til the next night. Like he thought he could sneak back in and I wouldn't notice he'd been gone.

Well, I'm not as dumb as he thinks I am. I waited and waited, getting angrier every minute. Then that next night, I heard a car pull up across the street. His buddies must've thought they'd make me think they were someone else, stopping at the neighbor's.

I went outside, stood at the door, and just waited for him to walk up. He looked like hell. I could see him trying to make up some lies as he walked towards the door.

I didn't say a word. As soon as he got close enough, I punched him a few times. Real hard. Really walloped him—he fell back and hit his head against the tree. He broke his nose and got a brain concussion.

Now I'm being accused of child abuse. What the hell—he's the one who caused it! I told him what I'd do if he snuck out!

In this case:

Skill #1: Decide (1) if *you're* ready to talk about it, and (2) if the other person is ready. If you were the father, *your* answer to the first question clearly is "no." Because of this, your son's answer to the second question doesn't matter. Even if his answer is "yes," this skill can't work unless *both* of you are willing to talk things over.

Skill #2: Talk to the person you're angry at (and keep everyone else out of it). You're letting your son know, all right. But *how* you're doing it is preventing the two of you from working on it. Without Skill #1, you can't solve anything.

Skill #3: Pay attention to their feelings (as well as your own). You're being controlled by *your* feelings. You don't have room for his. You can't make this work without Skill #1.

Skill #4: Find something in common. Nor this.

Skill #5: Depersonalize the situation. *This* skill could make a huge difference, *IF* your answer was "yes" to the first question in Skill #1.

Skill #6: Get to the *real* issue(s). The real issues are:

1. Your son shouldn't have sneaked out.

2. Your son shouldn't be using alcohol or drugs.

3. Your son was wrong.

4. But y*ou* are letting your *anger* control *your actions* — when *you* should be in charge of *them*.

5. *You lost control* — so much so, that you caused serious injuries to your son and also have to deal with legal issues.

6. Even though your son was "wrong," *you* made the problems much worse by *failing to separate FEELDO*.

Skill #7: Drop the grudge. The steps under "How to Drop a Grudge and Act Now" can help you get past your anger and get to the real issues with your son.

If you want to fix the relationship with your son, you'll have to go back to Skill #1 and make "yes" *your* answer to the first question. Your son's answer to the second question in Skill #1 *may* also be "yes." But it's more likely to be "no" for a while.

If you're *lucky*, he'll give you a chance to show him that *you* can *take charge of your own anger.* You'll have to show him you can make a S-P-A-C-E between what you *feel* and what you *do*—which is, by the way, what you hoped *he'd* do when you wanted *him* to stay away from his friends and their alcohol and drugs.

For your anger in general, the steps under "Letting Go of Grudges in General" will help. So will "Grieving." It will help you let go of your false belief that *real men* blow up. You'll have to drop your grudges for your own sake. And if you want to fix things with your son, you're going to have to drop your grudges for his sake as well.

When you can answer "yes" to the first question in Skill #1, and your son can either answer "yes" to the second question *or* at least be willing to listen to you, you have *all* the *real issues* listed above to talk about.

Start with real issues (4), (5), and (6). How *you* lost control and blew it. This will help you do Skill #3, pay attention to *his* feelings.

Of *course* you're right, in principle. You warned him, but he snuck out anyway. *Your rage is a natural feeling* in this type of situation.

But you *failed* to separate FEELDO. You *failed* to make a S-P-A-C-E between what you *felt* and what you *did.* You *failed* to stay in charge of your anger. You let your *anger* take charge of *you.*

If you want to start to fix the relationship with your son, take these steps:

1. Sit him down.

2. In a calm voice, tell him that *you* blew it, *you* lost control of your anger, you are deeply sorry for hurting him, and you will *never* let your *anger* control *you* again. (You *MUST* make sure this last statement comes true—for *both* his sake and yours.)

3. Tell him you will *make up* in any way you can for hurting him. This means you will have to show respect for him and his feelings at all times. You'll have to talk things over by making a *S-P-A-C-E* between what you *feel* and what you *do* when you get angry. You'll use the seven skills to do this.

4. Tell him you will take whatever legal punishment you get for abusing him. *Admit* and *accept* what you did—which is very different from "why" you did it or what you "meant" to "teach" him. *Own*

what you did. *Show* your son that a *real* man *takes responsibility* for what he does. (Make sure, of course, that you *do* all this.)

5. *Only after* talking about what *you* did wrong, can you talk about him sneaking out or his using drugs and alcohol in general. You—and he—may want to put a few days between the talks about *your* actions and the talks about *his*.

6. When you talk about *his* actions, use the same seven skills you should use when you're angry.

Father and daughter

I think of myself as an open-minded kind of father, you know, wanting my daughter to tell me the truth about what's going on.

But I do have my limits. When I found out she was pregnant—at 15 years old, if you can believe that—I blew up.

I told her I'd rather see her dead than be the slut she is.

I slapped her too, good and hard. I asked her what the hell she thought she was doing, living in our house, letting us pay for her slutty half-undressed clothes, and acting like a whore. You'd think she was in one of my porn magazines! No wonder she's so popular with the boys!

Let me tell you, as soon as I find out who the father is, he'll get it from me too. Wait till I get my hands on him!

In this case:

Skill #1: Decide (1) if *you're* ready to talk about it, and (2) if the other person is ready. If you're the girl's father, it's clear your answer is "no" to the first question. Your daughter's *would have been* "yes" to the second question, because *she's* already trying to talk to *you*.

Skill #2: Talk to the person you're angry at (and keep everyone else out of it). You're talking to the right person. But *how* you're talking to her will keep it from working. You can't use this skill without Skill #1.

Skill #3: Pay attention to their feelings (as well as your own). You're letting your anger *control* you. You aren't able to deal with her feelings at this point. *How* you're talking to her is making it worse. You can't use this skill without Skill #1.

Skill #4: Find something in common. Or this one, either.

Skill #5: Depersonalize the situation. *This* skill is what you need the *most* right now. Your daughter didn't aim her pregnancy *at* you. She came to you for help. It's about *her—not* you.

Skill #6: Get to the *real* issue(s). The real issues are:

1. Your daughter's pregnant.

2. She needs your help.

3. You're out of touch with teenagers' sexual behavior today.

4. You're angry enough to wish she was dead.

5. You *failed* to make a S-P-A-C-E between your anger and your actions.

6. You *lost control* of your anger. You're letting *it* control *you.*

7. Your involvement in pornography is hurting your relationship with your daughter. It's also hurting your relationship with your wife, women in general, men, *and* yourself. See "A Note about Pornography and Anger," below.

Skill #7: Drop the grudge. The steps under "How to Drop the Grudge So You Can Act Now" will help you get past your anger and focus on what *your daughter* needs.

If you want to fix your relationship with your daughter, you'll have to answer "yes" to the first question in Skill #1. You'll have to apologize for putting *your anger* ahead of *her needs.* You'll have to say you're sorry for not listening when she tried to talk to you. You'll have to say you're sorry for saying you wish she was dead. You'll have to follow all the steps in "Father and son," above.

Later, the steps under "Letting Go of Grudges in General" will help you give up your false belief that your daughter is still a little girl. *And* that *real men* lose control of their anger.

A Note About Pornography and Anger

This may sound strange. But pornography has a real impact on anger. This father's use of porn may be part of the reason he got so lost in his anger.

Porn *overtakes the* healthy, natural feelings about sex. And about children becoming sexual adults. *And* about daughters being sexually active.

In a healthy setting, the father could have helped his daughter grow up with a better sense of herself. And with a deeper understanding of why she might be acting in such a blatant, sexually provocative way.

But this father has used porn. Long ago, porn taught him to see young girls and women as sexual *objects,* not as *vulnerable people.* He lashes out—and even *hits*—his pregnant daughter because she triggered his memories of the sexual *objects* he's seen—and used. He thinks he *owns* her. That's *one* way porn had something to do with this father's angry reaction.

Another way is that a boy's first view of porn makes a lasting impression on him. Dr. Judith Reisman, author of many books and articles on how porn affects families, says that a boy's first reaction to porn involves *much more* than just a sexual turn-on. It *also* includes guilt, fear, shame, and other adrenaline rushes. The problem, according to Dr. Reisman, is that starting at a young age, men *learn*—from porn—to take *ALL* adrenaline rushes that are associated with girls or women (and sometimes boys) to mean *sexual* feelings. *Even when the anger, fear, guilt, or other adrenaline-pumping feelings have nothing really to do with sex.*

This means that maybe *part* of the father's problem is that his natural guilt or fear or shame about his daughter brought up all the guilt, fear, shame, and adrenaline rushes he associates with porn. Instead of being a worried father, maybe he took his adrenaline rush to mean he was the *jealous* or *jilted* father.

Or—maybe porn taught him it was okay to have sex with his daughter. Maybe he *was* jealous and jilted. Maybe his use of porn made him confused about *how* he felt about his daughter.

So another way porn may have had something to do with his angry outburst is that *anger*—another adrenaline rush—is the only way he knows how to deal with these frightening and confusing feelings.

Husband and wife

My wife and I had it pretty good for a while, but then she decided to get a job. I don't know why, because we have what we need with just me working. And I think a wife and mother should stay home. But she got real moody and nagged me about it for a long time, so I went ahead and gave her permission to get a job. It had to be close by, and she had to work only with women, you know, for safety reasons.

Well, that was just the beginning. The next thing was, she decided she should save a little of her money in her own account. I thought this was kind of silly, especially because all these years, all of my money went to us, the family. But I know she never really had anything of her own, so it didn't seem like such a big deal.

Then, after a while, she got bored and got another job elsewhere. I didn't even know she'd been looking. But it was a sales job, and some of the other salespeople were men. This bothered me, and once in a while, say during lunch, I'd stop by to see her at work, just to make sure things were okay.

And they sure looked okay, until suddenly, one day, bam! Just like that, she decides she wants a divorce. What would my family think? My friends? My co-workers? Sure, I have my faults like everyone else, but a divorce? I was shocked.

And I was furious, also. I knew it was one of those salesmen, even though she denied it. I tried real hard to find out—I pinned her against the wall, I slapped her, I made her tell me who it was. She kept claiming it was no one, just her own need, whatever that means.

She even said it was my fault, because I've hit her a few times. You know what? I only hit her when she does something that deserves it. It's not my fault, it's hers. If she'd gotten that straight, there never would have been any problems.

So you see what a little independence can do to a woman. I'm not done, you know. I'll find out who it is. I have a private detective on the case right now. And when I find out who it is, they'll both wish she had never left.

In this case:

Skill #1: Decide (1) if *you're* ready to talk about it, and (2) if the other person is ready. If you're the husband, your answer to the first question is "no." That makes it impossible to work on anything, even if your wife's answer is "yes" to the second question.

Skill #2: Talk to the person you're angry at (and keep everyone else out of it). You're focused *only* on how *you* feel. This skill won't work without Skill #1.

Skill #3: Pay attention to their feelings (as well as your own). You're too wrapped up in *your own* feelings. You're too closed to care about *hers.* This skill won't work without Skill #1.

Skill #4: Find something in common. You're interested *only* in what *you* want. This skill won't work without Skill #1.

Skill #5: Depersonalize the situation. You are *so* focused on *yourself* that you don't even realize your wife has her own point of view! If you depersonalize a little, you'll see that at least *one* of the reasons she left has to do with *your actions* towards her.

Skill #6: Get to the *real* issue(s). The real issues are:

1. You *abused* your wife when you hit her.

2. You want *control* more than *love.*

3. You see women in *limited* and *stereotyped* ways.

4. You made your "home" a *prison* to her.

5. You can't see how you look *to others.*

6. You're *closed* to others' ways of thinking or being.

7. You blame her job, her independence, and the so-called "other man." But the *real* reason your wife left is *how you treated* her.

Skill #7: Drop the grudge. You *won't* be able to do this, unless you can answer "yes" to Skill #1 and be more open to others' feelings and points of view. If you were open enough, "How to Drop the Grudge So You Can Act Now" could help *every time* you got mad at your wife. These steps would make you able to slow down and make a S-P-A-C-E between your anger and *what she really wanted or needed* from you.

And, if you were open enough, "Letting Go of Grudges in General" would help you give up your outdated beliefs that women exist only to serve you.

Anger and *shame*

It was graveyard shift. Some officers thrive on this shift. Others, like Officer X and myself, "volunteer" once every year or two.

I'm driving. It's about 3 a.m. This is drunk-watch. I hated drunks. My mother was an alcoholic, as was my grandmother. I felt a low simmer of resentment when I had to deal with these citizens. At one time, I liked throwing them in jail. By now, though, humiliating them had lost its shine. They all smell alike and they all say the same things. They were angry, manipulative, whining drunks.

Officer X observed a yellow Corvette get on the freeway ahead and alerted me. I accelerated to about 90 mph to close the distance. Traffic is extremely light. The Corvette started to pull away. I accelerate to about 120 mph and close a bit. Even with light traffic, I'm driving at the edge of my abilities. The Corvette pulls away momentarily, then slows to 110. I pull in behind at 110+ and "light" him up.

Officer X is bracing himself. It's been a short but wild ride. My adrenaline is pumping. I remember lights being brighter and colors vivid and my well-oiled hypervigilance deactivated as we pulled to the narrow right shoulder. My vision was narrow and too focused.

Ordinarily, there should be communication between the two partners on how to proceed in this dangerous situation. What level of tactics should be used, etc. This did not occur, because I was pumped.

I approached the Corvette on the left side. A tactical error and extremely dangerous. First, I had to stand in the traffic lane, due to the narrowness of the right shoulder. Second, indications were that this was not just another speeder. This situation called for a cautious approach where we might stay behind the cover of our car and use the public address system to talk to the violator, with his back to us.

We didn't do this.

The driver looked up at me and said, "What's the problem, Officer?" with a stupid grin on his face. I did not think this was a joke.

I don't remember much after this. I do remember flashing back to some locker room bravado I'd heard. One of my comrades was reporting how he'd pulled some guy out through the driver's window. I was sizing up this driver to see if I could pull him out through the window. I remember being surprised at his weight and that he wasn't fitting very well through the window. His head and shoulders outside with me and the rest somehow stuck. His screaming in fear.

I let go, opened the door, and dragged him down the traffic lane, stopping between his car and the police car.

Once he was on the ground in front of me, I had no idea what to do. As I think back now, I was shocked and sort of wondering how we got here.

At that moment, Officer X grabbed me and gently told me to stop. He turned to the violator, picked him off the ground, and dusted him off. He firmly warned the man not to speed, and apologized—not with words, but with body language and touch. He put his arm around the man and helped him back into the Corvette.

I felt enraged. I also felt shame about losing control of what I was doing.

In this case:

Skill #1: Decide (1) if *you're* ready to talk about it, and (2) if the other person is ready. If you're the officer telling the story, you're clearly not ready to talk to anyone. You're too lost in your own anger. *Your anger is controlling you.*

Skill #2: Talk to the person you're angry at (and keep everyone else out of it). Even if the driver wanted to talk it over, it takes *two* of you to make things work. And you *can't* talk things over, anyway—your anger is in charge of you right now.

Skill #3: Pay attention to their feelings (as well as your own). This skill won't work without Skill #1.

Skill #4: Find something in common. Neither will this one.

Skill #5: Depersonalize the situation. *This* skill is important to you right now. Right now for three reasons:

1. You *took* everything too personally already. Right now for three reasons: you lost control and let your anger take over. You let the driver "get" to you.

2. You acted too personal *because* you let the driver get to you. You did what you did *because* you let the driver's actions mean something about *you*.

3. You felt ashamed later because you lost control. Taking things personally *makes* you lose control. Especially of your anger.

Skill #6: Get to the *real* issue(s). The real issues are:

1. The driver was speeding *way* too fast.

2. The driver *might* have been drunk.

3. You, as the officer, had a personal grudge against drunks.

4. You assumed the driver was drunk. You let him *get* to you—*personally.*

5. You got *so* angry that you lost control of what you did. Your anger was ruling you.

Skill #7: Drop the grudge. You need to use the steps under "Letting Go of Grudges in General." Your grudge against drunks is too close to the surface. It's too much in control of you.

No-win situation

In this type of crisis, a police officer's goal is to prevent the suspect from killing the couple the suspect has at gunpoint. But the cop has other responsibilities too, so it's not as clear as it may sound.

For example, if I shoot and kill the suspect, this would remove the risk to the couple. But some people may see this as "police brutality." That makes me angry.

On the other hand, if I "just" injure the suspect, the cost of medical treatment and a trial would cost the taxpayers more money than burying him—and there still could be a risk of him killing the couple even though he's injured. That makes me angry too.

And back at headquarters—if I "only" injured the suspect instead of killing him, some of my fellow officers would see this as weakness on my part. They wouldn't praise me for saving the suspect's life. They'd avoid me and treat me as less than a man.

Not that they would come out and say I should have killed him. No, they wouldn't say the word "kill." They'd just refuse to look me in the eye. That makes me angry too.

And then, I have my own anger to deal with. Anger about the fact that anything I did in this type of situation would be wrong, from one angle or another.

In this case:

Skill #1: Decide (1) if *you're* ready to talk about it, and (2) if the other person is ready. If you're the officer speaking, you're *not* angry at another *person*. You're angry about the *circumstances*. But you can *still* use these skills to help you think through the problem.

Skill #2: Talk to the person you're angry at (and keep everyone else out of it). This is inside your own mind. Or, talk to someone who's willing to just *listen*.

Skill #3: Pay attention to their feelings (as well as your own). *Your* feelings are all that matter right now.

Skill #4: Find something in common. This is not an issue.

Skill #5: Depersonalize the situation. *This* skill can help save your sanity. You want to depersonalize *without* shutting down your feelings. The depersonalizing means that *you didn't cause* the problem. *And it's not aimed* at *you.* The problem is something you have to find a way to *deal with.*

Skill #6: Get to the *real* issue(s). The real issues are:

1. Your *human* side and your *role* may sometimes conflict with each other.

2. There *is no* one "right" answer. *You* have to decide what's the best thing to do.

3. This calls for *both* your *head* and your *guts.* Your *mind* and your *feelings.*

4. No matter what you do, some people will disagree. Some will treat you badly because they disagree.

5. You have to choose. You have to accept the problems that may come with your choice.

6. You have to do what *you* think, and feel, is right.

Skill #7: Drop the grudge. Whatever choice you make, *accept* it. Also accept its problems and limits. But *drop* it, once you've made the choice. *Avoid* going over and over in your head about it. Be *kind* to yourself about it.

The steps under "How to Drop the Grudge So You Can Act Now" will help. So will "Letting Go of Grudges in General" and "Grieving."

This is a real dilemma for heroes in desperate situations. Is someone a *man* because he's tough and "gets" the "bad person"? Or is he a *man* because he values life no matter whose it is? Is he *manly* because he doesn't let feelings like compassion get in his way? Or is he *manly* because he does? *You* have to decide for yourself what a *real man* should do in this type of crisis.

* * * * *

Taking Charge of Your Anger

A lot of things out there can make you angry. Righteously so.

Now you know the skills to use, to take charge of *your* anger like a *true man* instead of a wannabe. To stay in charge of yourself when someone's angry *at you*. You know how to *feel* your feelings—and then take steps to decide on the best thing to *do*.

Only a *real* man has the guts to both accept his feelings *and* take charge of them. One law enforcement officer spoke for *all* real men when he said:

> In my judgment, there is a huge shadow hanging over the law enforcement community—the total and complete suppression of emotion that is encouraged and expected in our front-line officers. I believe emotional expression is seen as "loss of control"—which is unfair to the officers.
>
> Control is everything. Control the scene, control the prisoner, control the crowd, control yourself. And I don't disagree with the importance of control. The problem is after the incident—when emotions could safely be released and dealt with. Yet there is nothing like this. Wash up, change clothes, go home.
>
> After a while—about five years, maybe—I could easily deal with anything that came my way. Never feeling anything. Laughing at tragedy. Good cop, handling anything.
>
> But there was that shadow. The lack of feelings doesn't fit well at home. It doesn't help your family. It doesn't go well with your friends. It leaves an emptiness in you.

You fill in the rest.

This is true of many jobs. And many men.

You can *feel*—and then *decide*. You can make a S-P-A-C-E to choose your actions. You can *feel* angry—and then *do* the right thing anyway.

Like a *whole* man.

Images of Angry Men

Each of these illustrations by artist Johnny Lewis (see page 127) relate to a story in this book. They show how intense anger can be. And how ugly it is when there's no s–p–a–c–e between what you *feel* and what you *do*. Feelings are natural and real. You have no control over what you *feel*. But you *can* control what you *do* when you're angry.

These men *didn't*. You *can*.

1. Army captain in Korea abuses his girlfriend.

2. Guy in a bar explodes in anger.

3. Crew member's favorite jacket is thrown into concrete for no reason at all.

4. Angry employee sabotages his boss's computer.

5. Angry traffic officer on the verge of rage.

6. Performance review provokes anger.

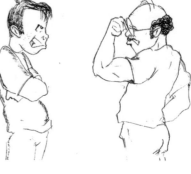

7. Special treatment of colonel's wife causes anger.

8. Angry father abuses his son.

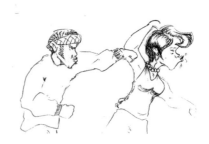

9. Pregnant teenage daughter infuriates her father.

10. Husband loses control over his newly employed wife.

Index

Anger Management Resources

THE FOLLOWING RESOURCES are available from Impact Publications. Full descriptions of each, as well as downloadable catalogs, video clips, and excerpts for many at www. impactpublications.com. Complete the following form or list the titles, include shipping (see formula at the end), enclose payment, and send your order to:

IMPACT PUBLICATIONS
7820 Sudley Road, Suite 100
Manassas, VA 20109
1-800-361-1055 (orders only)
Tel. 703-361-7300 or Fax 703-335-9486
Email: query@impactpublications.com
Quick & easy online ordering: www.impactpublications.com

Orders from individuals must be prepaid by check, money order, or major credit card. We accept telephone, fax, and email orders. Some titles are available on the GSA Schedule.

Qty.	TITLES	Price	TOTAL
Featured Title and Other Books By Author			
_____	Angry Men	$17.95	_____
_____	Angry Women	14.95	_____
_____	Anger and Conflict in the Workplace	15.95	_____
Pocket Guide (64 pages, 3 7/8″ x 4 7/8″)			
_____	Anger Management Pocket Guide	$2.95	_____
_____	Anger Management Pocket Guide (25 copies)	62.85	_____
_____	Anger Management Pocket Guide (100 copies)	207.00	_____
_____	Anger Management Pocket Guide (1,000 copies)	1,770.00	_____
Anger and Rage Management Books			
_____	Anger Control Workbook	$22.95	_____
_____	Anger-Free	15.99	_____
_____	Anger Management for Dummies	22.99	_____
_____	Anger Management for Everyone	17.95	_____
_____	Anger Management Sourcebook	21.95	_____
_____	Anger Workbook	16.99	_____
_____	Anger Management Workbook for Men	12.95	_____
_____	Anger Workbook for Teens	15.95	_____
_____	Anger Workbook for Women	21.95	_____
_____	Angry All the Time	17.95	_____
_____	Beyond Anger: A Guide for Men	15.99	_____
_____	Cage Your Rage for Teens Workbook	15.00	_____
_____	Cage Your Rage for Women Workbook	20.00	_____
_____	Cage Your Rage Workbook	25.00	_____
_____	Calming the Family Storm: Anger Management for Moms, Dads, and All the Kids	16.95	_____
_____	Freeing the Angry Mind	21.95	_____
_____	Getting Control of Your Anger	27.95	_____

_____	Healing the Angry Brain	16.95	_____
_____	Letting Go of Anger	16.95	_____
_____	Managing Teen Anger and Violence	19.95	_____
_____	Mind-Body Workbook for Anger	21.95	_____
_____	Mindfulness for Teen Anger	16.95	_____
_____	Pathways to Peace Anger Management Workbook	31.95	_____
_____	Rage: A Step-by-Step Guide to Overcoming Explosive Anger	16.95	_____
_____	Responding to Anger: a Workbook	14.95	_____
_____	Stop the Anger Now	21.95	_____
_____	Transforming Anger	15.95	_____
_____	The Verbally Abusive Relationship	15.95	_____
_____	When Anger Hurts	16.95	_____
_____	When Anger Scares You	22.95	_____
_____	You Decide About Handling Your Anger (book/workbook/CD)	39.95	_____

Violence Prevention

_____	Comprehensive Violence Prevention Video Library Series	$995.00	_____
_____	Please Stand Up! A Violence Prevention Curriculum	179.99	_____
_____	Surviving Domestic Violence	17.95	_____
_____	Violence Against Women	169.95	_____
_____	Violent No More	24.95	_____

DVDs and Treatment Programs

_____	Beyond Anger Curriculum With DVD	$195.00	_____
_____	Beyond Anger & From the Inside Out Curricula With DVDs	475.95	_____
_____	Beyond Trauma: A Healing Journey for Women	595.00	_____
_____	Cage Your Rage Program (for Inmates)	769.95	_____
_____	Changing Men: Unlearning the Behaviors of Domestic Violence	169.95	_____
_____	Dealing With Anger: A Violence Prevention Program for American Youth	225.00	_____
_____	Handling Anger and Frustration DVD	99.95	_____
_____	Hands Down: A Domestic Violence Treatment Program	68.95	_____
_____	Managing Anger and Rage: The Niagara Falls Metaphor Video Workbook Program	139.00	_____
_____	Manhood and Violence: Fatal Peril	149.95	_____
_____	Pulling Punches: A Curriculum for Rage Management	495.00	_____
_____	Real Deal! Anger Management for Adolescents (DVD Program)	279.99	_____

Special Value Kits

_____	Anger and Conflict Management Kit	$734.95	_____
_____	Cage Your Anger, Rage, and Violence Kit	903.95	_____
_____	Change Your Attitudes and Behavior K it	243.95	_____
_____	Domestic Violence and Abuse Kit	699.95	_____
_____	Managing Your Angry Self Kit	99.95	_____
_____	No More Bullying Kit	399.95	_____
_____	Peace Conflict Resolution Series	669.95	_____

Ex-Offender Re-Entry Resources

_____	Mindfulness: A Practical Guide to Awakening	$25.95 _____
_____	99 Days and a Get Up	9.95 _____
_____	99 Days to Re-Entry Success Journal	4.95 _____
_____	Best Jobs for Ex-Offenders	11.95 _____
_____	Best Resumes and Letters for Ex-Offenders	19.95 _____
_____	Beyond Bars	14.95 _____
_____	Chicken Soup for the Prisoner's Soul	14.95 _____
_____	The Ex-Offender's 30/30 Job Solution	11.95 _____
_____	The Ex-Offender's Guide to a Responsible Life	15.95 _____
_____	The Ex-Offender's Job Interview Guide	13.95 _____
_____	The Ex-Offender's New Job Finding and Survival Guide	19.95 _____
_____	The Ex-Offender's Quick Job Hunting Guide	11.95 _____
_____	The Ex-Offender's Re-Entry Assistance Directory	29.95 _____
_____	The Ex-Offender's Re-Entry Success Guide	11.95 _____
_____	Houses of Healing	15.00 _____
_____	How to Do Good After Prison	19.95 _____
_____	Jobs for Felons	7.95 _____
_____	Life Beyond Loss	20.00 _____
_____	Man, I Need a Job	7.95 _____
_____	Picking Up the Pieces	20.00 _____
_____	Quick Job Search for Ex-Offenders	7.95 _____
_____	Serving Productive Time	14.95 _____
_____	Support Programs for Ex-Offenders	29.95 _____

TERMS: Individuals must prepay; approved accounts are billed net 30 days. All orders under $100.00 should be prepaid.

RUSH ORDERS: fax, call, or email for more information on any special shipping arrangements and charges.

SUBTOTAL _____

Virginia residents add 6% sales tax _____

California residents add ____% sales tax _____

Shipping ($5 +8% of SUBTOTAL) _____

TOTAL ORDER _____

Bill To:

Name_____ Title _____

Address_____

City _____ State/Zip _____

Phone ( )_____ (daytime)

Email_____

Ship To: (if different from "Bill To;" include St. del. address).

Name_____ Title _____

Address_____

City _____ State/Zip _____

Phone ( )_____ (daytime)

Email_____

PAYMENT METHOD: ❑ **Purchase Order** #_____ (attach or fax with this order form)

❑ **Check** – Make payable to IMPACT PUBLICATIONS

❑ **Credit Card**: ❑ Visa ❑ MasterCard ❑ AMEX ❑ Discover

Card #														Expiration Date		
Signature							Name on Card (print)									

Angry Men and Women

BESTSELLERS!

Angry Men: Managing Anger in an Unforgiving World (2nd Edition)
Lynne McClure, Ph.D.

#2684 Shows men what triggers their anger as well as how they can take charge and gain control of their anger. Men see themselves in true stories from law enforcement officers, military men, and others who lost it because their anger took over. Includes seven easy-to-use practical anger management skills. Forewords by Lt. Col. Dave Grossman and Ronald L. Krannich, Ph.D. 144 pages. 2018. ISBN 978-1-57023-397-5. **$17.95. SPECIALS: 10 copies $145.95; 50 copies for $627.95; 100 copies for $999.95.**

Angry Women: Stop Letting Anger Control Your Life!
Lynne McClure, Ph.D.

#2685 Women let anger hurt their self-image, narrow their choices, limit their careers, and destroy their families. Their anger often leads them into depression, eating disorders, and destructive relationships. This book shows women how to take better control of their lives. Designed to be both self-directed and instructional, it includes easy-to-use practical, down-to-earth skills to reclaim control of their lives. 144 pages. 2004. ISBN 978-1-57023-206-0. **$14.95. SPECIALS: 10 copies for $119.95; 50 copies for $524.95; 100 copies for $747.50.**

The Anger Management Pocket Guide: How to Control Anger Before It Controls You!
Ronald L. Krannich, Ph.D.

#9100 This inexpensive guide offers invaluable tips on controlling anger, from identifying myths, triggers, and costs to joining anger management classes, forming a support group, finding a therapist, and even acquiring a loving pet. Filled with self-tests, examples, activities, tips, and techniques for creating a new anger-free you. 64 pages. 2015. ISBN 978-1-57023-352-4. **$2.95. SPECIALS: 25 copies for $62.85; 100 copies for $207.00; 1,000 copies for $1,770.00.**

Managing Teen Anger and Violence
William Fleeman

#6271 Filled with personal stories and vignettes, the book helps teens identify anger as a problem, recognize how they use anger like a drug, find non-violent ways to experience personal power, learn to change abusive and violent behavior, focus on values and goals that support a non-violent lifestyle, identify and change attitudes and beliefs that keep them stuck, and develop a mission statemente. 230 pages. 2008. ISBN: 978-1-57023-276-3. **$19.95. SPECIALS: 10 copies for $159.95; 100 copies for $997.50.**

Pulling Punches

#3039 Designed for recovering addicts and alcoholics with volatile anger, rage, and relapse issues, this highly acclaimed three-part DVD series addresses the whole anger process: Understanding Your Rage, Tools for Managing Rage, and Anger Reduction and Long-Term Changes. Each DVD runs 35 minutes and includes a Counselor's Guide with reproducible worksheets. Ethnically diverse, includes real people, and is narrated by a recovering person. Complete program for **$495.00. SPECIALS: 5 programs for $2,395.00; 10 programs for $4,595.00.**

Managing Anger and Rage:
The Niagara Falls Metaphor Video Workbook Program
William Fleeman

#9165 Focuses on the critical link between anger, substance abuse, and relapse. Explains how anger and the relapse process are similar to a disastrous trip down the Niagara River and over the Falls. Demonstrates how understanding Cues, Triggers, and Choices can overcome the destructiveness of the anger/relapse process. 43-minute DVD and one master copy of a 13-page interactive journal/workbook. 2015. **$139.00. SPECIAL: 5 copies for $599.00.**